Jo Hawes decided at 7 years ol[...]
professional entertainment althou[...]
might mean at the time. This decis[...]
mesmerised by Eric Porter's portrayal of Soames in *The Forsyte Saga*.
Since he was a well-known Shakespearean actor she is delighted, all
these years later, to be working for the Royal Shakespeare Company
on *Matilda*.

She started her career at the age of 15 as a dresser at the Theatre Royal
Windsor after pestering for a job for two years. After training as a
stage manager at the London Academy of Music and Dramatic Art she
returned to Windsor as a member of the stage management team. After
18 months she was offered a job on *Annie* in the West End. As a stage
manager she worked on (amongst other productions) three further
musicals: *La Cages Aux Folles*, *The Pirates of Penzanze* and *On Your Toes*.

Since becoming a Children's Casting Director 17 years ago she has
worked on over 75 productions – mainly musicals in the West End
and on tour – for all the leading theatrical producers. These include *Les
Misérables*, *Mary Poppins*, *Oliver!* (including the most recent one at the
Theatre Royal Drury Lane), *Shrek* at Drury Lane, *Chitty Chitty Bang
Bang*, *The Sound of Music* and many other productions.

In 2010 Jo began a series of workshops, Masterclasses in the Art of
Auditioning. She had auditioned many children but felt that many of
them do not give their best because they have never been taught the
technique of auditioning. She travels all over the UK and has taught
many hundreds of children.

Jo is married to Tim Hawes – a professional trumpet player – and they
live in Berkshire with their children, two of whom are also in theatre.

Jo.hawes@virgin.net

C000000616

JO HAWES
CHILDREN IN THEATRE
FROM THE AUDITION TO WORKING IN PROFESSIONAL THEATRE

A guide for children and their parents

OBERON BOOKS
LONDON

WWW.OBERONBOOKS.COM

First published in 2012 by Oberon Books Ltd

521 Caledonian Road, London N7 9RH

Tel: +44 (0) 20 7607 3637 / Fax: +44 (0) 20 7607 3629

e-mail: info@oberonbooks.com

www.oberonbooks.com

Copyright © Jo Hawes 2012

Jo Hawes is hereby identified as author of this work in accordance with section 77 of the Copyright, Designs and Patents Act 1988. The author has asserted her moral rights.

This book is sold subject to the condition that it shall not by way of trade or otherwise be circulated without the publisher's consent in any form of binding or cover or circulated electronically other than that in which it is published and without a similar condition including this condition being imposed on any subsequent purchaser.

A catalogue record for this book is available from the British Library.

Goodnight Mr Tom artwork is reproduced courtesy of Shaun Webb Design.
Oliver!, *Mary Poppins* and *Les Misérables* artwork is reproduced courtesy of Sir Cameron Mackinstosh.
Matilda logo is reproduced courtesy of Denise Wood at the Royal Shakepseare Company.

ISBN: 978-1-84943-127-9

Cover design and book illustrations by James Illman.

Printed and bound by CPI Group (UK) Ltd, Croydon, CR0 4YY.

Dear Misha
Lots of love

Jo xxx.

To my Husband Tim
and our precious children
Thomas, Matthew, Charlotte
and
Rebecca

CONTENTS

Glossary   8

1. Introduction   11

2. Casting   13

3. My Experiences   16

4. Agents   21

5. Training   27

6. Masterclasses   32

7. Auditions   38

8. Parents   52

9. The Audition Day   59

10. The Waiting Room   65

11. The Audition Room   69

12. Funny Moments   79

13. Recalls   81

14. The Offer — 84

15. Licensing — 87

16. Breaching the Law — 95

17. Types of Theatre Productions — 98

18. Rehearsals — 100

19. Performances — 105

20. Chaperones and Tutors — 119

21. Bad Behaviour — 122

22. Touring — 126

23. Child Protection — 132

24. Superstitions and Ghosts — 139

25. Reflections from Children and their Parents — 141

26. A Final Word — 152

Appendices — 154

Acknowledgements — 163

GLOSSARY

THEATRICAL TERMS AND DEFINITIONS

Auditorium
Where the audience sit to watch the performance.

Automation
The method by which scenery is moved around the stage electronically.

Beginners
A call to the stage for the cast and crew 5 minutes prior to the beginning of the show.

Blocking
The moves actors make around the stage during the show.

Break a leg!
A theatre expression meaning 'Good luck!'

Breakdown
Information sent out to agents and other interested parties detailing the requirements for roles in a production.

Calling the show
Usually executed by the Deputy Stage Manager, he or she will sit in Prompt Corner with the prompt script and will give all the cues for scenery, lighting and sometimes actors.

Cast
The actors in a production.

Centre Stage
The middle portion of the stage floor.

Character
A person in a story played by an actor.

Choreographer
A person who plans and teaches dances.

Cobo
Tickets left <u>C</u>are <u>O</u>f the <u>B</u>ox <u>O</u>ffice.

Company Manager
The person in charge of the cast, company, crew and payroll in the theatre.

> **Stage Manager (SM)** – in charge of the stage.
> **Deputy Stage Manager (DSM)** – usually calls the show.
> **Assistant Stage Manager (ASM)** – assists with the running of the show and looks after props etc.

Costume Designer
A person who designs the costumes.

Cue
A signal that tells an actor when to speak or move, a lighting operator when to change lighting, or for scenery to move. It could be audible, a light or a hand signal.

Curtain Call
The end of the show when actors take their bows.

Creative team
The people who direct/choreograph/ musically supervise the show initially.

Director
The person in overall charge of the artistic side of the production.

Downstage
The area of the stage that is closest to the audience.

Dress rehearsal
A rehearsal as much like a performance as possible but without a paying audience. Sometimes 'open' when it is done in the presence of an invited audience.

Dry tech
A rehearsal during which the crew and stage management move the scenery around the stage.

Flys
The area above the stage which houses scenery.

Footlights
Lights at the front of the stage on stage level.

Front of house
The area in front of the stage used by the general public, e.g. auditorium, bars, foyer..

Houseseats
Tickets held by the Management for use by the Company and VIPs.

Get In
When the set, props, costumes, lighting is installed in the theatre.

Get Out
When all of the above is removed from the theatre.

Grid
The area above the fly floor that houses the equipment needed to fly scenery/lighting and so on.

Half Hour Call
Thirty-five minutes before curtain up when all actors must be in the theatre getting ready.

Improvisation
A drama that is not scripted

Safety Curtain
Also called an Iron – a barrier between the stage and audience in case of fire – it must be dropped in view of the audience at every performance.

Lighting Designer
A person in charge of the light and lighting equipment on stage.

Mime
A performance without words.

Monologue
A scene when only one actor speaks.

Notes
Comments made to performers/crew/ stage management to improve the performance.

Notice
Advance warning that the production is closing.

Offstage
The area of the stage that is not seen by an audience.

Onstage
The area of a stage where actors perform.

Producer
The person who arranges the financing of the play and is in overall charge of absolutely everything!

Prompt Corner
The place backstage from where the show is cued usually by the Deputy Stage Manager.

Prop (property)
An object used by an actor.

Proscenium Arch
A decorative frame around the stage's acting area.

Pit
The area, usually under the front of the stage, which houses musicians and from where the musical director will conduct the performance.

Press Night
A performance when the press come in to review the show.

Previews
Public performances given prior to the press night.

Quick Change
From one costume to another in a few seconds.

Read Through
Actors come together at the first day of rehearsal to read the play.

Resident Team
In charge of the artistic side on a day to day basis during the run.

Script
A play in written form.

Score
Music and lyrics performed in the production.

Set
Scenery

Set Designer
The person who designs the scenery for a production.

Stage Crew
People who move scenery.

Stage Directions
Instructions to actors.

Stage Left
The area of stage that is on the actor's left when facing the auditorium.

Stage Right
The area of stage that is on the actor's right when facing the auditorium.

Sides
Pages of script often used in auditions.

Sitzprobe
A rehearsal when cast and musicians meet for the first time and sing/play the show for the first time without set or costumes.

Stage door
The entrance to backstage

Sung Through Musical
A musical performance without dialogue (not to be confused with opera).

Technical rehearsal
A slow rehearsal for cast, crew, set, costumes, props, lighting, etc.

Thrust Stage
A stage that has audience members on three sides.

Truck
A platform on wheels or winches that moves scenery around the stage.

Upstage
The back of the stage.

Wardrobe
The room in which all costumes are maintained.

Wings
The areas each side of the stage out of sight of the audience.

O ver the years I have accumulated a great deal of knowledge and seem to be quite well known in my field. So as soon as a show featuring children is rumoured to be happening the emails start arriving, often before I have heard anything myself! Parents and children assume that I will be casting the production and I usually hope that I am. For me nothing can quite beat the feeling of being offered a job on a huge new musical. I consider myself extremely fortunate to have carved a career out of a hobby. For that is how I view it, a wonderful hobby that I happen to get paid for! In a world where many people do not enjoy their jobs, I think I am very lucky.

I think it is a privilege to be able to witness young professionals at the start of their careers. They really are following their dreams. It is fantastic to be part of a team that has cast a child in a leading role when that child has never performed professionally before and very satisfying to see a child secure a tiny part and gain so much confidence as a result. It is rewarding to hear of a child's huge improvement in their school work whilst being involved in a demanding show and, more rarely, it is also wonderful to be able to follow the career of a performing child who goes on into adulthood playing leading roles. I would not have wanted to miss any of that. I consider myself fortunate to have worked in many beautiful and famous theatres with an amazing array of talent both as a Stage Manager and a Children's Casting Director.

I have written this book in order to advise, guide and inform parents and children about the wonderful world of theatre from the audition stage to beyond the closing night. I have concentrated mostly on live, professional theatre. I barely touch on other forms of professional entertainment since nearly all my work has been in theatre, which I absolutely love. I hope parents and children will find it helpful and will also have a few laughs along the way. I suspect that my passion for this crazy business will be evident!

That is not to say that my job is easy or always fun. It involves hard work, long hours and aspects of it can be deeply unpleasant. Would I change it? Not for a second! I could not imagine doing anything else. What luck!

Months before I even start to cast a show, rumours will start to circulate with varying degrees of accuracy! These will come from parents and agents asking if I know anything about whatever show they have heard about. Sometimes I do but I may or may not admit it depending on the circumstances! Anything I do say will be taken as gospel so it is often better to say nothing.

Sometimes parents have heard that a show has been pencilled into a particular theatre. They often know things before I do. The *Oliver!* tour was pencilled into the Wales Millennium Centre months before I was able to confirm that the tour was indeed happening.

Sometimes I won't have heard anything at all and a producer will call me out of the blue to discuss his latest project. This is usually because they will be budgeting and must factor in the huge costs involved in employing children. The budget will be based on how many children will be appearing in each show and whether it is in London or on tour.

If it is a touring production, decisions must be made about whether the children will be toured or cast locally – sometimes it is a combination of both. We will discuss chaperones, tutoring, hotels, travel, rehearsal, the tour schedule and who is going to be directing it.

The costs of putting on a show featuring children are huge and it is logistically tricky to the point where I sometimes wonder why anyone would want to do it.

After this I may hear nothing for ages. Some productions may not go ahead for many reasons. The producer may have wanted a particular household name above the title who has turned it down or is unavailable. They might not be able to find a suitable theatre or the whole thing could be cancelled due to lack of investors.

However, if the production is confirmed, the casting process begins. I will speak to the director and send out a breakdown based on the requirements. A breakdown is a letter containing all the information that agents or parents need to know in order to make a decision about whether to suggest their client or child for an audition. Breakdowns are used for all productions and for casting both adults and children. I will send it to all of the agents on my database, to the website notapushymum.com and other casting websites that reach a lot of children. I will email any previous casts also, if applicable. Some children will be too tall and some of the boy's voices will have broken, but they might have younger siblings keen to have a try!

In the past, suggestions arrived by post but these days I take all photographs and CVs by email. They usually pour in and come from parents, agents and children. Sometimes parents in particular will test me on aspects of the criteria that I have set out:

- Can my daughter come even though the breakdown says boys only?

- My son lives in Birmingham – is that considered commutable to London?

- I am 15 and although you are asking for children up to 13 years old please may I audition?

- My son is only 5 and very mature for his age – could he audition even though you really want an 8 year old?

It is hard to be patient when I have gone to great lengths in the breakdown to be clear but I try, very hard, with varying degrees of success. Sometimes it is a very good thing that I am alone in my study!

Casting is a rewarding and frustrating job. We usually see lots of children but, even though we may have been through several rounds, sometimes we have to start all over again. Occasionally I worry about where I will find more children.

3

My experiences as
a stage manager, chaperone,
mother and children's casting director

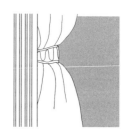

I have a wide range of experiences in and out of theatre to bring to this job. I trained as a stage manager at the London Academy of Music and Dramatic Art and worked for 18 months at the Theatre Royal, Windsor where I also performed. Some might say that playing a tap-dancing horse named Clarissa is not really performing, however! One night I went to a fancy dress party as Clarissa, walked up the drive and knocked on the door only to discover I was at the wrong house! But I digress…

My next job was as an ASM on *Annie* at the Victoria Palace Theatre in London's West End. Perhaps this was a hint of things to come as *Annie* features a lot of children! One of the orphans was a little girl from Wales named Catherine Zeta Jones. I subsequently worked on three more major musicals in London. I loved every minute of the various shows that I was fortunate enough to work on. However, it is difficult to combine this very demanding job with being a mother so I retired from stage management when I was expecting my first baby.

Whilst my two oldest children were little I worked in a number of theatrical offices, which gave me valuable insight into other aspects of the business. I worked for two adult agents, a publicist and for several years I was a Personal Assistant to a theatre producer who also ran a West End theatre.

In 1995 I was offered the opportunity to administrate the children in Cameron Mackintosh's production of *Oliver!* at the London Palladium. This was a complete baptism of fire! I had hardly licenced any children at the time and knew very little about the Children and Young Person's Act. I suggested that I worked from home because I instinctively felt that this was not going to be a 9 to 5 job. How right I was – my phone starts ringing at 7am and stops at midnight. After a few months I took on *Les Misérables* – then playing at the Palace Theatre, Shaftesbury Avenue and *Miss Saigon*, which was playing at the Theatre Royal, Drury Lane. Within 18 months I was working on 11 productions simultaneously!

After a few years I decided that I should leave my Ivory Tower temporarily and do some chaperoning in order that I could understand the difficulties of chaperoning. I worked on the set of *Harry Potter and the Prisoner of Azkaban* for a few days and I can honestly say that I have never been so bored in my life. Chaperoning is definitely not for me but it did give me a better understanding of the job. It taught me that chaperoning is not an easy option and best left to people who really enjoy it!

I have a chaperone's licence simply because we do not allow parents to watch auditions and, since I am always in the room, it makes sense that I do hold a licence. Occasionally I do chaperone on special occasions. Heather Miller was the head chaperone on *Mary Poppins*; she has worked with me for 17 years on many huge and complicated productions and is a brilliant chaperone. *Mary Poppins* was invited to take part in a specially written production to be performed in the grounds of Buckingham Palace during the Party at the Palace so I went along to help Heather. The Queen's garden was transformed into a wonderland of children's books and the special show was attended by Her Majesty and other members of the Royal Family. It was an unforgettable weekend!

I am also the mother of a performing child, my second son Matthew, and I am very grateful that I do have a true understanding of the huge physical and emotional commitment it requires. I have experienced at first hand the havoc it causes for family life, especially holidays. I can look parents in the eye because I know what it means to give 100% commitment to a show, which is what is expected.

I know what it is like to rush my son up to London at the last minute to cover whilst he has been in a show, however inconvenient it might be. I have sat in a waiting room while he sang his heart out in order to be cast in a part he so wanted. I have shared the successes and the failures. I have delivered Matthew to the Wycombe Swan Theatre for a performance of *Peter Pan* when it was snowing so hard that no sensible person would go out! I have also waited outside a stage door in the cold for the chaperones to bring the children out. I have mopped up the tears at the end of a run or if he has not been offered a part. Best of all I have experienced the overwhelming rush of pride the first time I watched my son take a curtain call in front of 2,500 people in *Oliver!* at the Theatre Royal Drury Lane which is, coincidentally, where my husband and I had met 27 years before.

Matthew's involvement in *Oliver!* had some very funny moments. It was his very first part in a production although, along with all my children, he has spent many hours in theatres during his life. On the very first day on the set we spent eight hours rehearsing the children into the opening scene which during the show only lasted fifteen minutes. Matthew was probably less than sensible in what he ate for his lunch and he was extremely excited. In the afternoon he was sick onstage during a rehearsal of 'Food Glorious Food'. He was carrying a metal bowl at the time and I asked him why he wasn't sick in the bowl rather than down the back of the boy in front of him! 'It's a <u>prop</u>, Mum!' he said indignantly. Fair enough, I thought, amused – he is the son of an ex-stage manager, after all!

Having my own child in one of my productions also brought its problems because as much as I wanted him to be like everyone else, he never could be. I warned him that at some point someone would say to him that he was only offered the part because of me. I knew that it was possible other children would be different around him and while I was agonising about all of that and wondering if we were doing the right thing, someone gave me some words of wisdom that put it all into perspective. Why should he not have the same opportunities as other children just because he is my son? That is so true and helps me when I am dealing with the children of performing parents who might also experience similar problems.

My older son, Thomas, appeared in *The Fix* at the Donmar Warehouse in 1996, which was a wonderful experience for him, especially because it was directed by Sam Mendes. Sam and I had discussed the role on the telephone and he described the boy to me not realising that he was describing my son exactly. Calvin Chandler Jnr should be 5 years old, blond with an angelic face. I remember saying to Sam that I had such a child in my own home! He replied that we would have him in the show then but I shot straight back with 'Oh no, he can audition with the others!' Thomas was keen to audition so I suggested him for it.

Sam had decided to cast initially by photograph so not wanting any favours I sent his picture in under an assumed name. He was picked along with half a dozen other boys to be auditioned by the Assistant Director who I already knew from *Oliver!* at the London Palladium. Unfortunately, he also knew Thomas but it was too late to do anything about that. Thomas was cast along with two other boys and he had a great time. They all did. He did lose out rather, though, as I asked Sam to let me know how he wanted me to divide up the first preview, press night and, since it was a limited run, the last night. 'You decide' was the reply. 'On any other production I would be glad to but not this one!' I explained. However Sam completely left it to me so poor Thomas didn't do any of the three special performances!

As a footnote to this Thomas decided to learn the saxophone after *The Fix* closed. He bought the instrument with his earnings and never acted professionally again. He is now working backstage in automation and loving it.

4

Agents

arents are often mistakenly told that I am an agent. I prefer to be on the other side, and am employed by the producer. I organise everything that relates to the children in a show. This includes finding the children in the first place, auditions, finding chaperones (and tutors if required), scheduling, licencing, liaising with parents, schools and local education authorities. I advise on all things legal and pastoral.

Sometimes parents contact me because the pestering by their children to do so becomes so intolerable that they have no choice! The conversation often begins 'My son/daughter has asked me to contact you and I know nothing about this but ....' Unfamiliar with anything to do with professional entertainment, they are thrown into a strange world where it is often difficult to break in and gather accurate information. Our business thrives on rumour, speculation and sometimes, more unpleasantly, gossip! I hope this book answers some of parents' many questions with accuracy.

Auditioning to the point where a part is offered is difficult enough, but that is only the start. Performing children have a very special, and to some extent, privileged existence which frequently sets them apart from their peers. Parents are often excluded from this world but are expected to be supportive. Their own lives and that of their other children take a back seat in favour of auditions, rehearsals and performances. The reality of such a huge commitment is often overwhelming. In common with having your first baby, it is impossible to imagine quite what it will be like until it happens!

As a parent of four children I know that there are very few things that children will encounter that their parents have not already done themselves. Parents can generally support and advise with knowledge even if their stroppy teenager doesn't want to listen! First day of school, learning to swim, making friends, falling out with friends, exams, senior school, further education, relationships, leaving home, jobs, getting married and having children themselves. These are part of life's experiences and everyone will go through at least some of them.

Auditions, however, are a very different matter and unless a parent is a performer themselves it is very difficult for them to help their child prepare. Auditions are not like an interview for a job and whilst parents might be supportive they might also inadvertently hinder by guessing what might happen – they do not really know so they are powerless to help. This is frustrating for the parent and sometimes detrimental to the needs of the child.

FINDING AN AGENT

What a minefield finding an agent can be. Many children do not have agents when they first approach me, but if they appear in a show, by the end of their run they will have decided in most cases that they would like to be represented.

I rarely approach adult agencies when looking for children – if such children do audition it will usually be because the agent has approached me. I think that children are better represented by a dedicated children's agency and nothing I have seen over the years in theatre has altered my opinion. Casting directors will not go to an adult agent in the first instance when looking to cast a child, unless the child already has several films under their belt, in which case their parents are probably not reading this book!

There are many agents in the UK, a few excellent ones, some that are perfectly good and unfortunately quite a lot of very bad ones. There are loads of agents in and around the London area but they are harder to find outside London. Many auditions take place in the London area which might mean parents who live a long way away are expected to travel, sometimes at quite short notice. This might not be very convenient and it is a big commitment in terms of time and money. It will also mean time away from school so an understanding head teacher will be essential.

Some agents are only interested in money and some do not have the connections necessary to secure auditions for the biggest projects. It is, apparently, quite difficult for a new agent to be taken seriously by casting directors. It is essential that parents research before signing on the dotted line. Children may have to audition so that the agent can decide whether or not to take them on. This is a good thing because it means that the agency is selective and does not take every child that approaches them. Needless to say it is very important that agent, parent and child all get on well to maximise a good working relationship.

Parents should not have to pay to have their child represented. The agents make their money by taking commission from any earnings, typically 10%–22.5%. The commission sometimes varies according to the nature of the job. Rates of pay for child performers are considerably lower in theatre than in film, for example. Many agents will want all their clients to have their photograph in Spotlight which is the directory of all performers, both children and adults. The photograph will be professionally taken: parents will be expected to pay for it and it should be updated annually. Many casting directors only cast by trawling through Spotlight. They look through the book or online and select children who they wish to meet with a view to casting them. Although it isn't compulsory to be in Spotlight, I would highly recommend it, otherwise an important source of possible work is lost.

If a parent has gone to the trouble of finding an agent for their child it seems strange that they then do the work for them. However this is often what happens. Having found an agent and signed up, parents come to me direct and do not tell their agent that they have done so. Meanwhile, the agent may have already suggested the child. If they have not it might be because they do not feel they are right for the role. If a casting director is approached about the same child by both the agent and the parent in the midst of booking in hundreds of other children they may not notice and give two appointments. Not only does this increase the workload but it fills up a slot that could be given to someone else. The casting director is obliged to go through the agent where there is one so will be in a difficult position if parents approach them of their own accord.

It is the agent's job to suggest their clients for projects for which they think they are suitable. If parents feel that their children are being consistently overlooked then they should in the first instance talk to their agent. It is demoralising for a child if they are consistently attending auditions and not getting very far, so perhaps the agent is just being selective. It could be that the parent has an unrealistic opinion of their child's talent or perhaps the agent has too many children on their books. Parents always have the option to move to another agent but it doesn't look good to keep changing. Bear in mind that if a contract has been signed and the child is fulfilling an engagement negotiated by the previous agent they will still expect to take the commission until the job is finished, even if a new agent is in place.

Of course if there is no agent, parents are at liberty to approach whoever they wish and the very best of luck!

- Send one good, clear, head and shoulders photograph by email or by post. More does not give any extra information. Any photos sent by post are unlikely to be returned due to the sheer volume received and the cost involved.

- Any information given in a letter should be short and to the point. Yards of information about previous work is not necessary and won't be read. Neither will reviews about previous roles.

- It is a mistake to direct anyone involved in casting to a performance on YouTube. It is usually really badly filmed and can sound dreadful. The result is that it will probably put off the casting director so will not result in an audition. I rarely watch anything on YouTube or other websites.

- If the height limit is 4 feet 4 inches it is pointless telling the casting director that the child is perfect for the role apart from the fact they are 2 inches over the height limit, in which case they are not perfect for the part! The criteria for all roles are set for a reason and such decisions are taken after thorough discussion which usually involves several people and is dictated by the script.

- Sending a CD or DVD is not necessary either unless it is specifically requested. The most important thing is to meet the child at the audition and hear them singing whatever has been asked for. Uploading such material onto the net, however lovely parents might think it is, really is a waste of time.

- An acknowledgment of an email from casting directors is possible but unlikely. It may be ages before parents hear anything at all and pestering is only going to attract the wrong sort of attention. Casting directors receive many approaches by parents and children. I probably receive at least one hundred a week if I am not casting anything and many hundreds if I am. It is not in our interests to ignore children because we must audition lots of children to give us the best chance of casting successfully. If children do fit the criteria it is quite likely they will be called in at some point so parents should try to be patient!

There are many options to consider and choices to be made when it comes to training, agencies and stage schools. Some agents are just that – agents. They do not offer anything other than representation, so it is up to parents to find good classes in drama, singing and acting to equip their child for the performing arts. The disadvantages are that the agent may not know what their client is capable of as well as one who both trains and represents children and therefore sees them regularly.

FULL-TIME STAGE SCHOOLS

Some agencies are attached to a full-time school which will be run in a similar way to other private schools, except the emphasis will be on performing arts training and may not offer other extra-curricular activities. They are often very expensive but some offer scholarships. Look out for details of scholarship auditions in *The Stage* newspaper (published on a Thursday) or by contacting the school direct. The week will be divided into academic work just like a 'normal' school and vocational training in many disciplines – ballet, tap, modern, jazz, singing, drama, acrobatics and so on. At the Sylvia Young Theatre School, for example, the academic side takes place on Monday, Tuesday and Wednesday and the performing arts are taught on Thursday and Friday.

The vocational side of the week at full-time stage schools will probably not include sport so consider whether that is a problem. They also vary in the quality of their academic education so it is important to check out results via Ofsted and by talking to other parents. Children in a successful stage school have to work incredibly hard because they must achieve in half the week what children in normal schools do in five days.

Sometimes children choose to board at a full-time stage school in London whilst parents live miles away back at home. Stage schools rarely have boarding on the premises so the children who cannot go home every night live with 'house mothers'. These are families whose children probably also attend the school or who may have done in the past. Choose the family with whom your child might stay with care and make sure they are going to be happy with them.

PART-TIME STAGE SCHOOLS

Agencies that are also part-time schools will have classes in the performing arts after school and at the weekends so that children can attend their own school as usual. The agency will know their clients well, which is an advantage when suggesting children to casting directors.

Which route parents take is entirely down to personal choice and all require careful thought and consideration. At all times the academic side is very important because as much as children may think they want to be an actor when they grow up, unemployment in this industry is high and it is challenging to work consistently. Qualifications are very important so parents should look into the pass rates at GCSE if considering the full-time option. Sometimes they are astonishingly good considering that a large part of the week may be spent working, auditioning or attending vocational classes.

Whether parents choose a full-time school or stick to mainstream education, I do believe this – child actors want to perform – it is so much part of them that they feel something is missing if they are not performing. They know that they must work hard academically because if they do not and a part is offered, their head teacher is likely to refuse permission when asked. The advantage to schoolwork is that the young actor has this wonderful incentive to keep up with it and they often do incredibly well in the classroom just because they are so motivated. Nagging about homework is just not necessary!

When considering all the various options keep in mind that it is perfectly possible for children to follow the part-time route and train at a full-time drama school after A levels. Our country is lucky to have several excellent colleges, both in and outside of London, which offer wonderful training from the age of 18. Even successful child actors do not necessarily go on to become adult actors, indeed many do not. However, Sylvia Young told me that of her pupils 65% go on to perform after they have left school and a further 15% stay in the media in some form or other – the rest go on to normal life! I am sure this is an unusually high percentage which I can only attribute to the fantastic quality of the training there and the fact that the children who attend really want to work in the performing arts and nothing else will do!

WARNING!

Sometimes children or parents are approached by a person who may not be all they seem. Such people may befriend parents in the first instance and it may seem very flattering but be extremely careful. They may promise representation or a part in a film or show. This can happen if children are in a theatre production, for example, and more easily accessible because they have to arrive and leave by the stage door. A reputable agent or casting director is unlikely to make contact with parents by hanging around stage doors. Our children are precious and rely on us to make responsible decisions. On more than one occasion I have had to warn parents to walk away and have even taken out an injunction and informed the police about a particularly unsavoury character who I was sure was merely in the early stages of grooming. Do take advice, google, speak to people and do plenty of research. It is easy for parents to be carried away with promises, flattery and all sorts, so I cannot stress enough the importance of constant vigilance because we live in difficult times.

'ORDINARY' SCHOOLS

Schools vary a great deal in their attitude to the performing arts. They may have a thriving drama department but even so may not want their pupils to miss school to take up a part. Some schools love the whole idea and bask in the reflected glory of having a child on a famous stage or in a film. All schools will monitor the impact on school work when a child is working. Finding the right school is essential.

The decision to send a child to an 'ordinary' school brings important considerations. Choose with care and talk to the headteacher about their attitude to theatre and whether they will permit time off for working. Discuss the child's aspirations in detail before making a decision. If they are already attending school when they decide they want to perform it may be necessary to move to a more performance-friendly school. The head teacher may be more concerned with league tables than allowing her pupil to follow their dream. That is a very big decision though, so think carefully before jumping!

HOME EDUCATION

Another alternative is to home educate. This puts a great responsibility onto parents although home-educated children are not obliged to follow the national curriculum. Local education authorities have to be informed and they may or may not inspect. Over the years I have come across a number of home educated children working in theatre.

Be honest with school and do not be tempted to allow a child to take a sick day to attend an audition. If the school is supportive they will understand that parts are only offered after auditions have taken place and these very often happen in school time. Honesty is essential because part of the licence application is a school letter from the head indicating support. Once a headteacher has refused permission it is often difficult to persuade them to change their minds, especially if they really believe that allowing their pupil to perform would be detrimental to their education. Even if a parent decides to remove their child from the school the local authority might be sufficiently concerned to be unhappy about granting a licence. So careful handling of the whole situation regarding school is very important from the start.

Performing children do miss an amount of school – this is unavoidable. How much time will vary according to the demands of the production. Rehearsals invariably take place during school time but, certainly in theatre, once rehearsals are over and performances have begun the shows are in the evenings, apart from the midweek matinee. However, there may also be rehearsals for adult understudies or cast changes once the show is running so schools will expect to be informed of this possibility.

It is vital that children attend school whenever they can – even if they are only there for the first couple of hours, the tick in the register is so important. If they do not attend as much as possible there is the risk that the school will complain to the local authority who in turn may revoke the licence. Once an authority makes the decision to take this action it is very difficult to persuade them to change their minds. Always have an eye to the next job – if the head feels that one job has gone well, the parent has been supportive to school and the child has attended regularly then they may be happy to grant permission again.

6

Masterclasses

One day a little girl – only 7 years old – audtioned for *The Sound of Music* and was not recalled. On returning to the waiting room she cried in her mother's arms which, although very upsetting, is not unusual. A few minutes later I happened to be at the door of the rehearsal room when she and her mother were leaving so I asked the mother if the child had known what taking part in an audition involved – 'No, not really' she told me. I then asked the mother the same question of herself and the answer was the same – 'No, not really'.

That was it – I decided to see if there might be any interest in classes that would teach children and young people how to audition. I was inundated within a very short time, and not just from individual parents but agents too who invited me into their schools.

Auditions are the first, most basic hurdle through which all performers have to jump unless they are so famous that they are simply offered a part.

Between 1995 and the present day I have sat through thousands of children's auditions. It has often occurred to me that there is no shortage of classes for children in how to sing, dance and act, but very few stage schools or drama teachers offer classes in audition technique specifically. I have seen talented children not really giving their best because they did not know how to apply their talent in the audition room. Many adult performers find auditions challenging and they are just as frightening for a child – nerves can really get in the way.

Most of the auditions I have run over the years have involved a group of around twenty children in the room. They are faced with a panel of adults who have all the power and who hold their fate in their hands. The children sing in a group and individually and might dance or read as well. They are often unfamiliar with the process, anxious and nervous. They can be intimidated by the presence of the other children and are afraid of making a fool of themselves.

These days many shows feature children. Some of them run for a long time and must be recast every few months. Casting directors, creative teams and resident directors, whose responsibility it is to cast these shows, need the children to be able to audition to a very high standard – to put their nerves aside and really show them what they can do.

The masterclasses are designed to help children to be more secure at this first most significant step towards a part. They are organised and run like an average audition. I see about twenty children in a session lasting 1.5 hours. The children arrive and I give them a label with their first name written on it. Sometimes casting directors use numbers but I dislike that, finding it impersonal. I believe it is better for young children particularly to be called by their name.

The children stand in a line and they introduce themselves. I ask them all sorts of questions – have they been to an audition before; what is an audition; how do they feel when they are waiting to audition. They arrive nervous, which is what I expect, but by the end of the session they tell me that they are much more relaxed and feel more prepared.

I ask the children to bring a poem or monologue which they recite by heart. Later I divide them into groups and they perform a short scene that I hope they have not seen before. We sit in a circle and I ask them to tell the group of any experiences that they have had when they have attended auditions in the past and whether they were good or bad. I ask the children to practice talking about themselves and we discuss the vital things they need to bring to the audition – confidence being the most important.

I suggest to the children that they approach each audition as if it was a lesson rather than an exam. Auditions are often run by supremely talented individuals who have a lot of knowledge and experience and might have been performers in the past so they have a lot to give. They probably haven't forgotten what it is like to be auditioning and are usually very good with the children.

I ask the children to consider how the panel might be feeling – that we want them to perform well and do their best and that we are not waiting for them to make a mistake because we want to cast the roles. If we do not then we have to start again.

NERVES

It is normal to be nervous at auditions. Adult performers are often very nervous when they audition too: they want the job but also need to work because they have bills to pay and so there is much more riding on a successful outcome. That is not to say that children do not want the part as much as any adult but it is different for a child and it really should be fun.

Some nerves are helpful but the trick is to find a way to make them work and not to let them take over so that it is impossible to give a good audition. No audition is so important that it is the end of the world – there will always be something else to audition for and it might be for an even more exciting part.

Nerves can make children rush when saying a poem or monologue. I ask them to take a deep breath and try to slow down and remember that what seems slow is likely to be normal speed. During any singing, they must listen carefully to the piano. A good audition pianist will help out, even bashing out the tune quite loudly if necessary.

The majority of the other children in the room will be nervous too. The children might be afraid of making fools of themselves in front of the panel but they in turn are probably just as concerned that they might not cast the part. The panel are definitely not waiting for their young auditionees to fall flat on their faces!

Occasionally during an audition a child will be so nervous and overwhelmed that it is all too much and they burst into tears. If that happens I take the child back to the parent, let them calm down and suggest they come back in with the next group. They might find that knowing a little more of what to expect they do much better. I never want parents to force their child back into the room. Sometimes they appear really surprised when I bring the tearful child out, telling me they are usually so confident, so unfazed and had been looking forward to it all so much. I do not take much notice of comments like these since confidence in a familiar situation or singing and dancing in the sitting room to doting family members is nothing like the intense scrutiny of doing it in an audition room.

Very occasionally younger children might be so nervous that they have an accident on the audition room floor. I feel so sorry for children when this happens – it is so embarrassing for them. I learnt after the first time an accident happened that if a child asks to go to the toilet they should be taken straight away.

The children usually tell me that whilst sitting in the waiting room for their turn to audition the most common two feelings that they experience are of nervousness and excitement. Very few children tell me that they are completely confident with no nerves at all. So we discuss the importance of dealing with their nerves and using them to their advantage if possible. I also remind them that it is just as important that they do not appear to be over confident. We discuss their fears, which are usually that they are afraid of making a fool of themselves in front of a roomful of strangers.

The children often refer to the panel as 'judges'. I tell them it is not a competition, not *The X Factor* or *Britain's Got Talent*, and we are in fact directors – not judges. Such TV programmes are primarily entertainment and real auditions are not run with an eye to the camera and the viewing public beyond.

Throughout the class I do not comment on the acting ability of the children and neither do I talent spot. That is not what the classes are for – I am more interested in their presentation. I explain that I will comment on the things they do throughout the lesson and I will be happy if they make mistakes because if they do not there is little point in them attending. It also gives me the opportunity to talk about their mistakes to the class so they can all learn from each other. Better to make mistakes in my class than in the real thing.

During auditions for my productions I rarely see children who are over five feet tall or older than 12 or 13. This is because in theatre children need to look like children and almost always have to be under five feet, undeveloped and boys' voices must be unbroken. The classes, however, include 7–15 year olds and, occasionally, I also help young adults. The older pupils are very interesting and focused because they have usually decided that this really is the career for them and so are preparing for the audition that will start it all off, the one for drama school! I love working with the older teenagers.

I know from the excellent feedback I have had that the classes are very helpful for most of my pupils. Parents and sometimes children take the time to email me with their thoughts afterwards. Such emails remind me why I started the classes. I thoroughly enjoy being able to pass on years of acquired knowledge and experience to the children and it is very rewarding to hear about their successes afterwards.

I am in awe of anybody, child or adult, who is prepared to audition or indeed perform at all; I would not and could not do it to save my life and so I salute those that do. Good luck to them, and if I can help them in some small way that is terrific.

7

Auditions

An audition is a meeting attended by producers, directors, musical directors and choreographers. They meet performers to cast a play, musical, TV drama, commercial or film. It could be for a part that will involve working for a day, several months or even years and could be at home or even abroad. The audition itself may take anything from a few minutes to a few hours and may involve several recalls before a decision is made. Children may be asked to dance, sing, act, improvise, read from the script, interact with other children or adults or any combination of these.

If the role demands it, children may meet leading actors with whom they would be working if they are offered the part. The children in final casting for the role of William Beech in a recent production of *Goodnight Mr Tom* worked with 'Mr Tom' prior to being cast. Children may be asked to do a screen test for film or TV. Auditions are a nerve-wracking experience and when I was a stage manager I saw many adults in pieces beforehand, so it is not surprising children are nervous too.

Parents are often very nervous as well. Consigned to a waiting room, they often look to me as if they are waiting for a particularly unpleasant session at the dentist! More on this later, but it is important they do not transmit their nerves to their children.

THE FIRST STEP – FINDING OUT ABOUT AUDITIONS

This can be quite challenging if children do not have an agent but it is by no means impossible.

The two main types of auditions are:

- Open Auditions.

- Auditions by appointment – usually, but not always, through an agent.

Anyone can attend an open audition but it is important to make sure that children fit certain basic criteria such as height, age and indeed how far away from the theatre they live. Open auditions are usually advertised widely in *The Stage* newspaper, the *Evening Standard*, local press, on the internet or on the radio and the word also spreads quickly between children! The great thing about open auditions is that they can offer opportunities to complete newcomers which for me, and I imagine other casting directors, is very exciting.

I recall open auditions in 1996 for *Oliver!* at the London Palladium. A young lad came along who had only ever sung in his school choir. He was offered the title role and also went on to play it on tour. He later played Gavroche in *Les Misérables* in London and on tour. Had we not held open auditions at that time we may never have found him. Parents sometimes think that it is only possible to audition through an agent. I really don't mind whether the children have an agent or not as long as parents tell me.

The negative side of open auditions is that they are not by appointment but simply advertised asking children to turn up at a certain time. They involve many hours of waiting with several hundred other children and parents. I do not think that keeping children outside in the cold for hours is the best way for them to audition well, and have developed a system whereby everyone comes to a desk at the head the queue in order. They are then given a time to come back later in the day. If I think it is going to be a particularly good turnout I might even have another day organised and book children in for that once the first day is fully booked. The main thing is that everyone who turns up and who is within the various criteria for the part is auditioned. Turning children away is not an option – I always have the nagging feeling that on a day when we might only have time to see 150 children, it is the 151st child that might have been 'The One'!

Standing in such a long queue is intimidating for an inexperienced parent especially if they happen to be standing next to someone hell bent on giving everyone the benefit of their experience, not to mention their child's entire CV. Parents may be tempted to run away and not allow their child to go through the trauma of auditioning. Try to ignore it because it might just be worth persevering.

Parents often ask me in advance of open auditions if I know how many children will be there and what time they should arrive. I can only tell them that it is quite common for the first auditionees to arrive at 5am with chairs and a picnic!

However, a savvy parent might arrive at midday because very often, once the system is up and running, it might be possible to slip a child into a group during the course of the day. It is strange but sometimes parents queue up, are given an appointment and then they are never seen again! Odd, but it does happen.

ON ARRIVAL

The first job when I arrive with my team for a day of open auditions is to measure the children. I think it is better that they are turned away sooner rather than later if they are too tall. I use what has been nicknamed a Chip Stick (because I first used it when casting Chips for *Beauty and The Beast*) and it is marked with height limits that are the maximum for various shows. It is only 5 feet long because it is so rare for parts to be cast with children who are taller than that.

A child needs to look like a child so height is often critical. If I have to turn a child away parents often comment that they have seen the show and are positive that the children are actually much taller than the height limit given for the audition. Of course they are because it is in the nature of things that children grow and, much like buying new school shoes, we have to build in growing room!

It is extraordinary how many children, according to their parents, inexplicably grow two inches overnight! They might lean against the wall hoping I will not notice that their knees are bent so that they appear shorter. Parents are then very upset when I explain that the height limit is what it is and it would be a waste of time their child auditioning. I am often asked 'Can they audition for the experience?' to which I reply that when I have a queue of 1500 we do not really have the time to audition children just for the experience however much we might like to!

Next we give out numbered raffle tickets which tell me how many children are in the queue and also eliminates queue jumping. This usually works brilliantly, although parents have been known to go to the local newsagent to buy an identical book of raffle tickets in order to move up the line! The various tricks I have witnessed over the years never cease to amaze me.

I always ask the venue that we are using to leave the queue outside until I am there so that we do see children in the order in which they arrive. But on one occasion I arrived at a venue to find that a helpful theatre manager had let them all in. Fortunately we could see them all in the one day but it was interesting how many of them claimed that they were the first in the queue!

Open auditions are easy to attend and parents may soon find that they have got themselves into something they did not seriously consider. I have occasionally offered a part to a child whose parent gasps 'We didn't think she would get this far!' They promptly decide that they will turn the role down without really thinking about the devastating effect this might have on their child. Auditions are a rollercoaster of emotions and children have to work hard to gain a coveted role, often against stiff competition. Just when they have achieved their prize it is snatched away by their own parents. Additionally, for the team casting the role, they suddenly find that the child they had thought so perfect for them is no longer available. This is really exasperating.

So please keep reading and think carefully before setting off for any audition at all.

Once parents have decided to allow their child to audition for a part, they must be prepared for a great deal of waiting and some disappointments too. Parents should bring plenty to eat and drink and dress appropriately as they could be standing outside for some time. A sense of humour and loads of patience is essential. Before setting out make sure children are the right height, age and so on or, having finally arrived at the front of the queue, they may be turned away without singing a note! Arguing will not help. In the end it is up to the casting director who they will or will not see and they are bound by the demands of the role.

For their own sake I recommend that parents also check carefully on any other criteria before they embark on a long day of queuing. Producers often place restrictions on how far away from a venue the child lives. However much a parent might say that commuting to London from Timbuctoo won't be a problem, the fact is it will! It is very expensive and inconvenient to have children travelling long distances to perform in shows. In addition children must go to school as much as possible and for at least 15 hours a week. Travelling time seriously interferes with that. Children cover each other in performances and are sometimes called in at short notice, especially as there are very often no child understudies in the theatre. A child that lives within the M25 is obviously going to be able to come in faster than one who lives north of Birmingham. Whilst this may seem terribly unfair these decisions are based on practicalities.

The biggest problem with open auditions is that whilst we might make every effort to circulate accurate information, as it is passed from person to person details are missed or changed. I always take a laminated copy of any advertisement that we have placed with me so that I can prove that we have done our best. I have had a few very unpleasant encounters with parents over travel because coming to London from Aberdeen to be first in the queue usually involves an overnight stay and expensive travel. Whilst I have every sympathy I cannot see such children if the management requires them to live close to London. I probably only have a certain number of hours in which to audition everybody who does live close enough and I think it is very unfair on the team casting to have to audition children to whom we cannot make an offer.

AUDITIONS BY APPOINTMENT

Where auditions are offered through an agent they are usually, but not always, by appointment. Do not necessarily expect them to run on time either! It is always a good idea to double check the details since regrettably agents often send children for castings for which they are entirely unsuited. Since attending auditions often means missing school, not to mention the expense involved with travel, parents should be sure that their child is at least the right height and so on.

Once agents have made their suggestions, casting directors will give agents the details of the auditions including the time, venue and whatever script or song is to be prepared. The agent will confirm the arrangements with the parents, sometimes at very short notice, but they will be expected to drop everything and go! If parents turn down too many auditions for their child, eventually none will be offered. The reason for this is that casting directors sometimes limit the number of children they see because of shortage of time. Agencies may only be permitted to send one or two children. If they do not turn up when their agent may have several other children they wanted to send, it is very frustrating. Agents are very touchy about this because non-attendance will reflect badly on them and there is a risk that they will be seen as unreliable, and it is quite possible that casting directors will refuse to consider any of their children in the future. If parents cannot be bothered to attend an audition, the huge commitment involved in fulfilling any engagement is probably not for them.

Sometimes siblings attend auditions together and that places the casting team in a dilemma. Statistically it would be extraordinary for both children in one family to be offered parts in the same show at the same time. I have known it happen from time to time; and on one occasion to twins in the first cast of *Chitty Chitty Bang Bang* at the London Palladium. Years before this the same twins came to audition for the role of Molly in *Annie* on tour and only one of them was cast. If one of the siblings is recalled or even offered a part I just hope that their parents will make sure that the other is not left out and will have prepared both of them in advance for the possibility that it is unlikely they will both be cast.

The majority of agents will only suggest a few carefully selected children but others will email me what seems to be their entire client list. I always ask them to include each child's name, height, age and education authority. I very often receive a list with incomplete information or a few details that tell me quite clearly that the breakdown I so carefully put together has been pretty much ignored. I suggest to them that it might be an idea that they re-read the breakdown and resubmit their list.

Many children's agents have so many children on their books that I think it must be very hard to really know them. I also realise that parents do put pressure on the agents to send their children to audition whether they are suitable or not. It is not fair on the child or the team who are casting for agents or parents to send unsuitable children to auditions. It is awkward for children if they come into the room and they can see for themselves that they are too tall or too old because the rest of the children are 6 inches shorter or 4 years younger. It is also such a waste of everybody's time: the parent, the child and the casting team.

If agents completely ignore the requirements that I give them I am tempted to exclude their children from further auditions. Very occasionally I might turn children away at the door. The agents are usually extremely apologetic and often try to blame the parents by saying they had not been given accurate and up to date heights. This may well be true because unfortunately parents are sometimes economical with the truth because they are so desperate for their children to audition. Sometimes they think that to attend an audition irrespective of whether the child is suitable is great experience. In reality, it simply means that another child might have been refused an appointment through lack of time. I wonder why any agent, or indeed parent, would put their child through such an experience for absolutely no reason, especially when they might be missing school to do so. On such occasions as these I often go to the parents in the waiting room and explain why their child is not being recalled so that they understand – I can only imagine what they might say to their agents when they have a chance!

Too often children who clearly cannot sing at all are sent to audition for a musical. I have been known to write next to a child's name 'Does the agent know this is a musical?!' However, most agents are brilliant and take great care to send me appropriate children.

I know that agents often do not pass on more than the barest details to the parents of their clients so I always take the opportunity to give plenty of information at the audition itself, which is the first time I see the parents face to face. The initial audition form includes the dates of the production so that parents can see immediately if it is going to be a possibility for them if their child is cast. Even so parents do continue through the process knowing there is a clash. Once the child is cast they will contact me and explain how they are so sorry, they didn't think their child would make it through to final casting, they have a clash and it is only one day, etc. This really is not fair to the child or indeed the production. Parents who try this fail to understand that it is so important that I am even-handed when there a number of children in a show. If I agree to one child missing 'just one day' I have to agree to everyone's request. Parents often tell me that their child is really quick at picking things up but this does not take into account that however quick he or she might be the work still has to be taught to the child separately from the others who will already have learnt it. So if every parent demands the same for their child this could be half a dozen extra sessions on a show with a small number of children or one hundred and fifty on a show like *Oliver!*

It is detrimental to the rehearsal period for children to be missing and makes it so much harder for the creative team.

The recall letter is another opportunity for me to make sure parents are fully informed about the commitment – if there are several recalls I give the same details each time so that no one can say they were not told!

These days I do not often recommend advertising for children even in the out of London venues because it is very expensive and rarely has the desired effect. I prefer to spread the word through my contacts in each venue and I find that live radio interviews are helpful. I rarely hold auditions which are 'open' in the true sense of the word. This way of describing auditions is a bit confusing where children are concerned. For adults auditions are run in two ways – 'closed' where only invited actors who come through their agents are seen and 'open' when anyone can turn up on a given day and can hope to be seen.

Many children do not have agents – at least when they first approach me. It does not matter to me at all. Any child who contacts me, providing they fit the basic criteria, has exactly the same chance of being seen. Therefore the terminology 'open' and 'closed' does not apply to children as far as the way I cast is concerned. I receive many 'cold calls' via email and that is no problem – I welcome such approaches. All the programmes for the shows that I am casting include a box letting parents and children know that we are always looking for children and displaying my email address.

AUDITION VENUES

I have auditioned in many different buildings and, unfortunately, it is quite difficult to find venues that are welcome to children's auditions. Two spaces are required – one for the parents to wait, and one in which the children will audition. Children come in groups so the days are busy – sometimes we might see 350 children in a day – and they all bring a parent. So any venue must expect noise and crowds.

My preferred audition venue is the Sylvia Young Theatre School, which moved in 2011 from their premises in Marylebone to a fabulous new building near Marble Arch. We are made to feel welcome in gorgeous, light rooms while the parents wait in the canteen or a waiting room. It is perfect!

Based on the requirements, I like to gather as many children together as possible so that we have a good chance of casting the show in the first set of auditions.

AUDITIONS IN LONDON

London auditions often take place over several weeks and involve first rounds, recalls, final casting and the possibility of starting all over again if we find that we have not cast everyone. It is normal to see at least 500 children for a big show but far less for something smaller. Open auditions for a new show in London could attract a turnout of 1000 or more.

AUDITIONS OUT OF LONDON

These auditions are usually for touring productions where children will play locally to the venue. I email all my local contacts, which are considerable these days, and word also travels so I do have many referrals. This is great – the more the merrier. If I am worried about not finding enough children to audition (which I occasionally am in some venues) I will ask for some radio publicity to help out and such auditions are usually advertised in the local paper. The bigger venues –

Cardiff, Manchester and Birmingham for example – are not usually a problem and I expect a good turnout.

Regional auditions often happen over a weekend and are busy and tiring. They might consist of two long days of perhaps 9am–9pm. The casting team often come from their other commitments and it is not always easy to get everyone together. These occasions are really challenging for us and the children but it is rewarding to cast from beginning to end in two days. For parents it can be very draining and involves a lot of waiting around and a rollercoaster of emotions.

The Saturday will be first rounds and Sunday likely to be recalls. We aim to cast and offer by late afternoon on Sunday and at that point I like to have a parent's meeting. Out of London parents are inexperienced in this business and have usually had a long and stressful wait so are quite tired by the time we are ready for the meeting. They sometimes cannot quite believe that their child has been offered a part and frequently look completely shell-shocked.

Children who are cast regionally are expected to commute on a daily basis and so where they live is important and clearly stated in advance. I recall a child being cast in a show on tour in a main part. The mileage was given as 25 miles and the family lived over 50 miles away which, unusually for me, escaped my notice. Once the children started rehearsing the boy was doing a great deal of travelling and the director noticed that he was not learning his lines or doing his show homework. I was asked to speak to the mother who raged at me about the amount of travelling he was doing and how could we expect him to do it all when he was spending so much time in the car. I pointed out that it was her choice to be doing so much travelling since the advert had clearly stated the distances and that if he did not do the work required at home we would not be able to keep him.

Some years ago I was auditioning in the north east of England for local children to appear in a touring show while it was in that area. A girl auditioned and was offered the part. The licence was granted and everything was fine until I received a phone call at home one night from the chaperones after the show. No one had collected her. It turned out that she actually lived in London. This episode was particularly unpleasant, the girl lost the part and I nearly ended up in court even though I had applied for the licence in good faith. The driving force behind this breathtaking act of deception was her agent, aided and abetted by the family. These are the lengths some parents and agents will go to.

By law children must be licenced by the borough in which they live and if parents or agents pretend that children live elsewhere any licence will be granted illegally which, if discovered, will be withdrawn without notice. Apart from the fact that this is very inconvenient for the production, it is dreadful for the child who is the person most affected by the stupidity of the adults who are supposed be looking out for their best interests. Unfortunately the child is also the person who can do nothing to change any situation in which they find themselves and they are left really disappointed.

THE RACE RELATIONS ACT 1976

The requirements for a part when casting a show is always very specific and this can occasionally sit uncomfortably when taking into account the Race Relations Act of 1976. However there is a specific clause in the amended regulations in 2003 (section 4A, Clause 2a) which states as follows:

2) This subsection applies where, having regard to the nature of the employment or the context in which it is carried out —

(a) being of a particular race or of particular ethnic or national origins is a genuine and determining occupational requirement

This means that where *The King and I* requires South-East Asian children, *The Lion King* requires dark-skinned children, or any show in which both parents are seen will require the children to be of a similar skin colour, we can legally advertise for the specific look. I am always more than delighted when the parent of a child approaches me for a particular show for which they are obviously not suited (due to skin colour) and I can point them in the direction of something else I might be doing. In the end it all balances out.

Parents

Unfortunately, the pushy parent is alive and well and living in the UK. Thankfully they are the small minority but they do take up a disproportionate amount of time. Sometimes they make their presence felt at the very first audition and it is not unknown for the audition form to come to me with the initials MFH (Mother from Hell) already written on it – put there by a long suffering stage manager who has already had enough in the waiting room. This is not very flattering, and such mothers really do not help their children. Any mother who makes so much fuss in the audition is probably only going to get worse at the Stage Door and, unless the child is absolutely exceptional, coping with that parent is simply not worth the hassle.

There is a big difference between the pushy parent and the one who is inexperienced and needs lots of advice. It is a question of knowing the difference. Checking on arrangements and other practical information is fine but the audition stage is too early for parents to bombard any of us with loads of questions about minute details. Sometimes information is sent in advance by email. It should be read carefully as some of the answers may be there. Beware of asking other parents because they may not give correct information. Stage Door gossip is very unreliable and the bane of my life. A parent once asked me to write a letter denying all the rumours that were circulating. I would not know where to start.

It is very disappointing for parents if their children do not receive a recall but making a fuss about it will not change the outcome and will be very embarrassing for everyone, especially the child. All parents believe their child to be special and the best but that does not make them right for every part for which they audition.

After auditions I often receive emails from parents of children who were not recalled or cast asking why their child 'failed'. I point out that it is not an exam and that they might not have been cast for a multitude of reasons. The word failure is very misplaced and in this context is sending out quite the wrong message to the child.

Auditions seem to bring out the worst in some parents. They are often far more desperate for their child to be cast than their unfortunate offspring, who occasionally look as if they would rather be anywhere than in front of a panel of directors. One Musical Director I worked with used to begin each session by asking the children 'How many of you are here because you want to be here?' closely followed by 'How many of you are here because your parents want you to be?' It was staggering to see that each time around a third of the group would admit that they were only there because of their parents.

In the past a child came to the same audition three times in one day, wearing different clothes and looking increasingly awkward each time. When she failed to get a recall on the third attempt I let the mother know that we were quite aware of what she was doing and it really would be better if she took her daughter home! She did have the grace to look sheepish but I felt for the poor child.

Sometimes children do audition quite legitimately several times for a production over the period of the run. Some may not do too well initially. Eventually, though, they are offered the part they so want. Generally speaking though, sending a child to audition over and over again for the same show is demoralising if they are going to face rejection each time.

I often receive emails or telephone calls from parents anxious to tell me that their child is 14 or even older but is still under 4' 10" and could pass for a 10-year-old. It is rarely the case that a 14-year-old does not look 14 behind the eyes because the experiences of an older child are not going to be the same as those of a 10-year-old irrespective of height. They have probably reached puberty and although they may be quite short for their age they will almost certainly look mature. Girls look like the young women they are and boys voices deepen as they become young men.

Any producer that intends to cast children will want them to look like children, otherwise they might as well cast a young adult without the hassle and extra expense of licencing, chaperones and several teams to pay for. Maturity will shine through and it is very rare to be able to successfully cast an older child in a younger part. Personally I do not like to see adult performers playing children and for me it rarely works.

Casting teams are always worried about boys' voices breaking in the middle of the run. It is very difficult to recast in the middle of a contract with all the attendant cost of rehearsals and costumes but is also so upsetting for the young man who has to leave for no other reason than he is growing up. I have had to release several boys over the years and it is always difficult to tell them that they cannot do the show anymore because they are going through puberty. At a time when they are already conscious of all the changes that are happening to them this is highlighted in a very public and brutal way and they lose their role through absolutely no fault of their own. So we spend a considerable amount of time during auditions checking boys' voices so that we are as sure as we can be that they will be able to complete their run without mishap.

I had to release a boy from *Chitty Chitty Bang Bang*. His voice had matured quite fast and he was no longer able to sing the role of Jeremy Potts successfully. The producer called me on the morning of a matinee day to ask me to explain to the father that the two shows that day would be the last for him. I considered carefully whether I should tell him before the two shows or after – either seemed so cruel! On balance I decided that I would do it before the shows and I rang his father. He was so lovely about it and thanked me for giving his son the opportunity to say goodbye to everyone. Lots of his friends and family had watched his last performance and they had been grateful that they had been given the opportunity to do that. We lost a boy even more suddenly on *Oliver!* He performed Act I but was unable to continue after the interval. He and his family handled this very difficult situation with aplomb. It must have been so hard for him but he even stood in the wings for Act 2 and helped his understudy through the show. What a professional!

Some shows require songs to be sung in the chest voice and some in the head voice. Casting directors must cast children with chest or 'belt' voice with extra care or any girl with the voice of an angel may well end up sounding like a heavy smoker! There are many things to take into account when casting and it is rarely an easy process.

MANAGING EXPECTATIONS

Many of the problems that occur in auditions and in shows could be avoided if parents tried to manage their own expectations and those of their children. Parents can help their children so much by keeping their own and their children's feet on the ground. It is a fine line to tread between excitement and being realistic. Parents vary so much from the ones that loudly announce that they never expected their child to be offered an audition, a recall or the part to those who rush straight to the press the minute their child has been made an offer.

BE POSITIVE AND REALISTIC

During the audition process it is important for parents and children to keep a sense of perspective. Someone is going to be offered the part but the process might not be easy. It is a pointless exercise for parents to try to work out the odds if their child is lucky enough to get down to the final few because in almost every case directors do not take the best of the children on the day, they take the best. If that means starting all over again then that is what they do. If a child is eliminated it is very disappointing but it is important for the parent and the child to focus on the positive. Children can learn so much that they can take to the next audition.

MEDICAL CONDITIONS

I have come across a number of parents who are happy to conceal their children's medical conditions on the grounds that if we knew we might not cast them. They do have a point but they also take breathtakingly irresponsible gambles in the process, particularly in the case of children that live away from home. It is unfair on the chaperones if they are not acquainted with the full facts when in sole charge of a child whose parents might live a considerable distance away. Complete honesty is vital for the sake of the child because sooner or later such facts will be revealed anyway.

When I discovered by accident that a child had a medical condition that could have been serious for himself and others around him, I rang the mother to discuss it with her. Her response was 'I do hope you didn't think I was trying to keep it from you, Jo'. I replied 'Yes that is exactly what I think you were trying to do!' We had only discovered the problem because he was overheard talking about it to another child. I found it extraordinary that any parent could sleep at night when they lived so far away having concealed the full facts from the chaperone.

HOLIDAYS

It is very awkward if parents suddenly 'remember' that they have a holiday booked after their child is cast in a production. However much they might think that their child is completely irreplaceable the likely outcome is that he or she will have to be recast because it is just too complicated for directors to work round holiday commitments. Be completely honest from the start because otherwise the choices will be to either turn the part down or cancel the holiday.

Families must make sure that the commitment of being involved in any show is acceptable to everyone because for the period of the contract the job must come first. This may be easier said than done but it is a golden rule of having a performing child. It turns family life upside down and there is no doubt it is restricting. Children work on a rota but do not be tempted to go on holiday during days off or to ring in sick. Children will sooner or later give the game away and it is so unfair to put them in a position where they have to be careful what they say in the dressing room. I have caught out a number of children over the years and I am afraid such deception invariably leads to suspension or even termination of the contract. It is inconsiderate to the other families who will be required to cover, to miss shows for any reason other than genuine illness. Children have to do what their parents tell them but it is the children that are likely to be punished.

WHOSE DREAM?

Children should be following their own dream and not their parents'. This business is like no other and it is not right for everybody. It invades the soul but it is also full of rejection which many adults find difficult, so how much harder is it for a child? If they say 'I don't want to do this, Mum' then they must be allowed to make that choice. The saddest thing is seeing a child in the waiting room crying and a parent trying to persuade him or her to audition.

On the other hand, if a child is pestering to be allowed to audition for something then I believe they should be given that opportunity because the experiences are extraordinary. It is hard for parents to allow them to audition and for them not to be cast but parents can support, advise, listen, mop up the tears and delight in their successes. I was allowed to follow my dream and have not regretted it for a second – I believe that all children should be allowed to follow theirs. Indeed nearly five decades after I decided that I wanted to work in professional theatre I am still capable of great excitement when a new show is offered to me. If it is challenging, so much the better. The day I am offered a new show and fail to be excited by it will be the day I retire.

9

The Audition Day!

uditions do not usually happen in theatres. A rehearsal room is more likely and this is a good thing because staring across the footlights listening to a disembodied voice is, I believe, even more intimidating for a child than being in a room in ordinary light.

When casting musical theatre, it is common for children to be auditioned in groups – typically around twenty children at a time. The first rounds are often only 30 minutes per group so there isn't long for the panel to get to know the children. This is why they should not waste a second of their precious time in the room. Singing often takes place first with dancing and acting seen at the recalls. Sometimes each group might be seen for over an hour and singing, dancing and acting are all tested. The panel always want children to be as relaxed as possible so sometimes they will play a few games and make it all as much fun as possible.

Auditions for other things – film, TV and commercials – are quite different. Any script is usually given in advance and it is very important that children learn it as well as possible. It is quite common for these auditions to be videoed and then the film might be viewed later by the director or another creative person involved in the decision-making process. It is a very good idea for children to practice sight reading script out loud in case they are given something at an audition that they have not seen before.

Parents should bring drinks and snacks for any breaks that the children might be given. Try not to bring siblings if at all possible because space is usually limited; it is very boring for them and just adds to the stress.

PRETENDING TO BE CONFIDENT

The way children enter an audition room tells us a lot about whether they want to be there. Children should walk into the room quietly but with confidence even if terrified – if they manage to fool themselves into believing that they are brimming with confidence the panel will believe it too.

Remember that all the children auditioning have as much right to be there as anyone else. They are only in competition with themselves and the other children present are no more or less likely to get the part. If asked a question, they should answer it in a clear voice. Remember some theatres seat 2500 people and the audience must hear everything. Whispering to the floor so that even the people 6 feet away cannot hear is not going to convince the panel to offer a recall.

Over confidence is nearly as bad as being under confident. Resist the temptation to be too chatty – or indeed lippy; do not suddenly pipe up with inappropriate comments. Children should not be afraid to ask a question but should make sure to ask at the right time and very politely. They should never interrupt or fidget when another child is auditioning.

WHAT TO WEAR TO AN AUDITION

Children often wear completely inappropriate clothing when auditioning.

- All clothing should be comfortable and suitable for movement and sitting on the floor.

- Costume or anything resembling it is to be avoided. It tends to set children apart and often makes other children stare which only adds to the pressure and the nerves. It often causes raised eyebrows from the panel also. Many children turn up to *Whistle Down the Wind* in plaits and dungarees, *Mary Poppins* in pretty period dresses and *Oliver!* in Artful Dodger gear complete with braces. One child came to a *Les Misérables* audition in rags and carrying a broom! It very nearly cost her a recall. Only the fact that she had a great voice saved the day. I think that if children come attempting to dress like the character they or their parents are auditioning for they are actually saying that they think directors have no imagination and cannot see the child in the part.

- Wear clothing that is age appropriate. It should not be revealing, skirts should not be too short, midriffs should be covered. Suggestive logos are to be avoided and indeed any sort of logos are forbidden for TV castings for advertisements.

- School uniform is not ideal.

- Well-fitting footwear is essential. Flip flops, heelys, high heels, even Uggs are not suitable. Trainers or jazz shoes are best but do also remember to bring ballet or tap shoes if necessary.

- It is probably best not to wear jewellery.

- Hair should be tidy and long hair should be tied back so that the panel can see the child's face – particularly their eyes. It is distracting if children are continually pushing their hair out of the way.

- Children who try to audition wearing a hat are invariably asked to remove them because they sometimes hide their faces.

- Children who are auditioning for the role of a child will be expected to look like a child so wearing any sort of make-up is inappropriate and very unhelpful.

CHEWING GUM

Gum is not welcome in auditions, rehearsals or performances. The only thing that is needed in the audition room is a bottle of water.

THE ROLE OF STAGE MANAGEMENT AT AUDITIONS

Auditions are usually run on the day by a stage manager or chaperone who may or may not be part of the production. This person will be bombarded with questions most of which they cannot answer because they may not be connected to the production beyond their services on the audition day! Their job is solely to check in the children, collect forms which they will have given to the parents to complete, attach photographs and stick name labels to the children. They will be busy keeping the auditions running smoothly by ferrying children in and out of the rehearsal room and, most importantly, keeping the panel topped up with copious amounts of tea and coffee!

PUNCTUALITY

It is a cardinal sin to arrive late for an audition and is not helpful to the child who will be too stressed to give a relaxed and successful audition. Making excuses about the traffic, train or underground when the other nineteen children already in the room managed to arrive on time definitely does not make a good impression. Punctuality is very important and parents must leave plenty of time for travel.

Everybody is late occasionally and sometimes it really is unavoidable, but whatever the excuse it is not helpful to walk in five minutes after everyone else. Most people will try to accommodate latecomers but sometimes the auditions are a process and to come in halfway through might not be fair on the child because they may have missed vital stages along the way.

- Leave plenty of time and plan to be there 15 minutes earlier than the appointment so that there is time to visit the toilet. It is always better not to have to ask to leave the audition room if possible. Parents need time to complete any paperwork and children can try to focus on the coming audition.

- Take detailed directions and contact phone numbers in case the worst happens.

- Late arrivals will be seen if it is appropriate to do so but don't be surprised if this is not possible. Having a screaming match with the long-suffering person at the desk is not going to help!

THE AUDITION FORM

Parents are usually given a form to fill in on arrival which will request personal details including their address.

Agents do not like such details of their client to be given on these forms but I have been caught out several times with children not living where I have been told they live which is why I do like to know, especially if distance from the venue is important to the producer.

Sometimes parents do not give their agent on the form which does annoy agents because if they have done the work and sent the child to the audition it is only fair that, if they are cast, the agent receives the commission.

Parents should have telephone numbers and email addresses handy to complete these forms accurately. Basic measurements are sometimes requested also so keep those up to date, especially height, weight and shoe size.

PHOTOGRAPHS

Any photos that are asked for should be clear, head and shoulders images without make-up and clearly named. Holiday snaps in bikinis on the beach are not suitable and neither are pictures of the entire family and the dog. If asked for a passport-sized picture don't take a glossy 10 x 8 – it will almost certainly not be returned so save the money!

If asked to email a photo make sure it is small enough that it won't take hours to download and don't send ten photos in a variety of different poses.

Be careful how any photographs are perceived. I was once shocked to find a photo of a child draped on a bed in my inbox – it is irresponsible to send such a picture across the worldwide web to a stranger. Parents must remember that their offspring are precious and should be especially protective of daughters.

10

The Waiting Room

The place where parents wait for their offspring while they are auditioning is invariably inhabited by certain types of parents who are usually, but not always, mothers –

1. The Interrogator

This parent will fire questions at the person in charge of running the auditions who may not know much anyway! She will also interrogate her child after the audition about every minute detail including who was making the decisions which the child will probably not remember. Bombarding children with questions after an audition is a waste of time because they are unlikely to have any idea of how they did and are probably starving!

2. The Peeping Parent

Parents are excluded from auditions for very good reasons. This parent, despite of the best efforts of people like myself to block up any windows or doors, will manage to find a chink through which to watch their child auditioning. On a number of occasions I have moved parents away from doors so many times that in complete exasperation I will eventually explode through the door almost knocking them flying in the process! I do not allow parents to watch auditions, because I never want to hear a parent say to their child that they could have done better – with all due respect to parents they do not know what the directors are looking for.

3. The Nervous Parent

This parent will bite their nails down to the quick, pace up and down and jump a mile in the air every time the door to the waiting room opens.

4. The Show Off

This parent will tell anyone who wants to listen (or even if they don't!) the various achievements of their child and try to intimidate the other parents into the bargain. Actually the only job that is important is this one.

5. The Gossip

This parent will delight in making up anything they don't know and hand out loads of incorrect information. Inexperienced parents will take anything said as the truth.

6. The Complainer

This parent will complain about the amount of time they have been waiting for their child to be seen, about the amount of time their child has been in the audition room, the lack of information, anything that they can think of. They do not realise that they would be doing their child and everyone else a big favour if they just sat down quietly with the newspaper and a coffee.

7. The Wanderer

This parent will disappear when their child is auditioning and occasionally not return until well after their child has finished her audition, if at all. Auditions can be very tedious and nerve-wracking for parents with a lot of waiting around but if asked to wait they must do so for their child's safety and well-being. It is awful for a child if they have worked hard over a period of time and then they are not asked to stay in the room for further auditioning. They are taken back to the waiting area wanting to have a good sob and their parent has disappeared.

8. The Pushy Parent

This parent will have bribed their child into attending the audition and will be shocked when they come out crying and saying they do not want to be there. She will probably try to get the child to go into the room again whether they want to or not and will eventually take them home and give them a good telling off.

9. The Inexperienced Parent

This parent will sit quietly, completely intimidated by everything and listen to anything that is being said and believe it.

10. The Absentee Parent

This parent will send their child to the audition by themselves without putting in an appearance at all. Although there is no legislation to cover auditions this does cause problems for us because children should not go home unaccompanied.

11. The Sensible Parent

This parent will sit quietly and know that this is not the only audition in the world and that their child has just as much chance of getting the role as any other. If the child is not successful this parent will reassure and tell them that there will always be another audition and not to worry.

In short, the waiting room is a difficult place to be! Take a newspaper, a drink and settle in for what might be a long day.

Performers, both adults and children, attend far more auditions than they are offered jobs. This can be very demoralising if it is allowed to be. It is a great help if the children can look on the positive side all the time, or the unpalatable truth is that they might not survive in such a cut-throat industry. It is hard at 10 years old or so, but they have entered an adult world where they are expected to behave as the young professionals they are. Cat fights at the Stage Door between parents are very undignified and might even impinge on their child's chances of future success. Sadly there are times when the actions of the parent outweigh the talent of the child – it is rare but it happens.

The Audition Room

How many people are auditioning the children will depend on the type of show and whether it is a first casting or a recast. When a show is new or being cast for the first time the audition process tends to be a bit different from any recast a few months later. On a big musical there are likely to be several rounds with an associate or resident director, casting director, musical director, a choreographer and pianist. After the initial rounds there will be a final casting when they will also be present together with the show's main director and possibly the producers. This can be quite intimidating – at a recent final casting session of mine there were at least twenty people in the room, and that did not include the children. The children must focus on the job in hand and just concentrate on the one or two people that will be talking. Children should try to not worry about anyone else. By that stage they are likely to have an excellent chance of being cast so should try hard to remember how well they have done to have seen off so many other children.

Later when the show is running and it is time to recast the children there are usually fewer rounds and less people involved in the casting. However for main parts the director and producer may still come to the finals.

Children can only do their best at auditions – they cannot do more and should try to enjoy it as much as possible. The directors want them to be as good as they can be because they want to cast the roles. Sometimes parents complain after the auditions that their children have only sung two lines and how can anyone tell what they are capable of from that. The directors know exactly what they are looking for. The child may simply be too young, too old, too small, too big, too dark, too blond – there could be loads of reasons why a recall is not given and sometimes none of them are to do with talent. Each audition is a new opportunity to learn – often the directors have so much experience that it can be a great lesson and huge fun.

Other children may be a distraction during the audition either consciously or unconsciously. Children should try not to take any notice and simply concentrate harder.

Auditions such as I have described are not like the ones on the television which are designed primarily as TV entertainment. Theatre directors and producers do not want to make children cry. I believe that TV auditions have, to some extent, contributed to the poor turnout that we occasionally find these days at open auditions because parents do not want their children to be upset by an audition panel. Although we do occasionally have tears they are usually because the child feels completely overwhelmed by the whole experience or desperately disappointed that they have not done as well as they feel they could have. Ridiculing a child's performance is not a good way to get the best out of anyone and particularly not children. In my long experience of auditioning children none of the teams I have worked with have had any intention of humiliating children. Quite the reverse, in fact. I have been incredibly fortunate to work with some of the loveliest and most talented directors, choreographers and musical directors in the country and indeed the world. They simply want children to be as good as they possibly can be and they work hard to make the auditions fun.

It is very rewarding when I receive emails after an audition from a parent telling me how much their child enjoyed the experience and even more so if they were not even recalled. This is a job well done! I like my auditions to be organised, to run on time and to be fun for the children.

SMILE!!!

A smile goes a long way and might distract the panel's mind from any mistakes. Eye contact is also very important, as hard as it might be with total strangers. Sometimes it is difficult for younger children in particular to look at the panel so they should at least try to focus on a point and try not to let their eyes wander all over the place.

ACTIONS

Sometimes children are taught actions to songs from long-running productions in advance by their dance schools in the hope that this will help them secure the role. In my experience the opposite can be true. Generally speaking directors would much rather see children sing the song with their feet rooted to the spot and with lots of expression in their faces. All actions and movement will be taught in rehearsal. The purpose of the audition is to find out who is right for the part, not whether they are already rehearsed.

Do not be intimidated either by the child standing next in line who has learnt the moves – take no notice.

THE IMPORTANCE OF LISTENING!

This is one of the most important things to remember – that notes given to a child in an audition might be useful for all children. So they should listen carefully to everything that is being said. Gazing blankly into space is not going to be helpful.

The panel only have such a very short time to make their decisions – sometimes there may be twenty children auditioning in a 30-minute slot so it is important for children to make an impression for the right reasons. Look them in the eye when speaking to them because they won't bite!

It is essential that children remember that once in the room, how they behave when other children are auditioning is every bit as important as how they audition themselves. Children that talk when they should be silent, fidget or stare at other children while they are singing, simply attract attention for all the wrong reasons. Sometimes this can even make the difference between being given a recall (or even the part) and not. If the panel have to keep telling someone to keep still or stop talking I can be fairly sure that a recall for them is not likely. Auditions can be extremely boring if they are taking a while and involve listening to other children singing the same eight bars a number of times. However, remember that this is also true of rehearsals so the panel will be looking for children that can really concentrate.

BE PREPARED

Children may be asked to bring something with them to the auditions or be sent something in advance. Be sure to prepare thoroughly and learn it by heart if possible. However, children should not be 'coached' in advance by anyone because someone else's way of doing it may not be the same as the director's. Children may find it difficult to change the way they deliver dialogue if they have been coached in a particular way and this may put them at a disadvantage.

Some directors ask the children if they know anything about the character they are auditioning for so if there is an opportunity to see the production (if it is already on) that would be useful.

Occasionally there will be no clue in advance as to what children may be asked to do. Sometimes this is so that the director can assess how quickly they pick up new material. They should listen carefully and ask about anything that they might find confusing.

Even if children are told that nothing needs to be prepared in advance it is sensible to have certain things ready just in case. I would suggest a poem, a monologue (neither of which should be more than a couple of minutes at most), a song, a joke and the ability to talk about themselves. It is easy enough to practice on parents and is useful to have a few facts ready in case the director asks such as name, age, favourite subject at school, siblings, pets, favourite food or even most hated food. If any of that raises a laugh so much the better.

Script is often given at auditions to read there and then. It should be read several times but unless the child has a photographic memory they should not even try to do it from memory. An audition is not a memory test so hold the words but away from the face so that it is visible and look up as much as possible. Fiddling with clothes is a sure sign of nerves and can be quite distracting for the casting team. I recommend practicing poems at home in front of a mirror so that children can learn to keep hands and arms still. Children should try not to put their hands in their pockets or cross their arms though – boys in particular sometimes do this – it looks as if they don't really care whether they are there or not.

MAKE MISTAKES WITH CONFIDENCE

Although it is important to do what is asked as well as you possibly can, mistakes are common at auditions and it really isn't a problem unless they are repeated many times. If children forget lyrics they should make them up or sing to 'La'. Similarly with dance steps carry on confidently and smile. The panel may have been looking at someone else at the time! Routines are usually done more than once so not to worry – just correct it for the second attempt. Never be afraid to ask to be shown again. Remember this is an audition, not a performance.

SONGS

- Very often children are told what they must sing at auditions. If so they must learn it thoroughly and by heart. It might be something from the show for which they are auditioning or perhaps something that everyone knows but which is in a similar style. There will always be a reason why a certain song has been chosen. For example 'Somewhere Over the Rainbow' is often chosen because there is an octave leap in the first two notes. Almost anything might be required.

- Being able to bring a song of choice is terrific because it means that it can be something that suits the voice perfectly – take advantage of this and choose carefully.

- Auditionees should make sure that their song is one that they enjoy singing.

- Any song should not be too long.

- Try to practice with a pianist a few times prior to the audition and ask that the music is put onto a CD for further practise at home. The CD could also be taken to the audition if there isn't going to be a pianist present.

- If taking sheet music for a pianist to play, make sure it is organised in the right order and on good paper that will stay on the music stand without falling across the keyboard.

- Whilst the pianist may well be able to transpose, it is much better if the music is in the right key.

- a cappella (unaccompanied) singing can cause problems for children so the use of a pitch pipe might be good so that at least the first note is correct. However, in general I think that a cappella for children is to be avoided since it puts quite a lot of extra pressure on them.

- Songs should be appropriate to the age of the child. I have seen children appear with songs that are far too old for them – even suggestive in some cases – and whilst this might be amusing at home in front of uncritical family members it will look dreadful in front of an audition panel. A 10-year-old flirting with the panel is embarrassing for everyone.

- Older teenagers could have a choice of songs if possible.

POEMS / MONOLOGUES

As with any song, make sure that any poem or monologue is suitable and not too long; two minutes is sufficient. This doesn't sound long but it really is plenty especially when there might be nineteen other children in the room waiting. Be prepared to be stopped before the end and don't worry about that if it happens. It may be that it was so great the panel have heard enough. All pieces should be very well prepared and word perfect. Try not to choose anything too intense. I have recently heard one or two monologues about disease, death and the afterlife and whilst they were beautifully performed it did rather dampen the atmosphere in the audition room.

COACHING

If children are given material to learn before any recall they should not be coached in how to say it – by parents, drama teachers or anyone else, however well-meaning. Parents should let children work it out for themselves and confine any help to assisting them to learn the words. The director will soon tell the children what he wants them to do.

DYSLEXIA

Dyslexic children should not be afraid to say so – I have sat down with children on several occasions and gone through script that has been given on the day. They have usually compensated for their dyslexia by having fabulous memories. Directors will understand and make allowances. Remember there are many famous and highly successful dyslexics! Some of these might surprise and inspire.

Tom Cruise

Robbie Williams

Roald Dahl

Walt Disney

Fred Astaire

Keira Knightley

Darcey Bussell

Dyslexic children sometimes achieve great things in theatre. They are often very bright but find it hard to express themselves in the written form. The confidence they acquire from performing often helps them in ways that may be unimaginable at the start of an engagement and their schoolwork is often greatly improved as a result.

I recently took issue with an education authority who announced that they were preparing to refuse licences for work that they deemed of no educational worth. I sent the following letter to *The Stage* newspaper:

> As the Children's Casting Director for over 75 West End and Touring productions over the last 16 years, I am very concerned about the recent decisions taken by a London borough regarding child licencing. Not only do they wish to charge for the processing but they are also considering refusing to grant licences for children if the work is not considered 'educational'. Who is to say whether or not it is educational? The effect on a child of taking part in a professional production cannot be overestimated. Performing improves their confidence and whilst there is often an impact on the amount of time spent in school, such children often work harder at their academic studies because they realise that if they do not, permission to participate in the production will be refused by the head teacher. I regularly receive letters from parents whose children have recently performed in one of my productions anxious to tell me what a wonderful experience they have had, how they have grown up – blossomed even – and how they have kept up with their school work and done well in exams. Performing children learn valuable lessons about working in a disciplined environment. They must be punctual and committed. They work with dedicated and talented performers, directors, musical directors and choreographers and they are able to experience at first-hand just how dedicated they must be in order to carve out

a career for themselves. They have to work hard at the audition stage to be cast in the first place and they are passionate enough to want to jump those hurdles. These things are life lessons. At a time when many young people are uninspired and unmotivated, how short-sighted to punish children by denying them these fantastic opportunities. How soon will it be before this attitude spreads to other local authorities? In the meantime the children of the borough in question may not be cast because producers may not take the risk that the licence application might be turned down.

I sincerely hope that they will reconsider.

Imagine the child that has auditioned several times for a part, kept up with his school work knowing he must to keep his teachers happy and is then offered the part. His licence is refused because someone in a local education authority office has decided that performing is a worthless experience. Is he then going to go back to school as motivated as he was? I very much doubt it – he will be crushed and unless he is very unusual he is going to think, 'What is the point, I simply will not bother'. Who could blame him, and what a missed opportunity! I believe that, although school work is very important, it is not the only thing that matters in life and some children thrive on the practical experiences that are derived from performing.

12

Funny Moments

Auditions have given me headaches, laughs and stress in equal measure over the years!

One day, as I was walking up Tottenham Court Road on my way to *Beauty and the Beast* auditions, I said to my assistant that it was always my fear that I would arrive at a venue to find no one waiting to audition. We turned the corner and…there was no one waiting to audition! The publicist was standing in the foyer at a loss. These auditions had been advertised in every single McDonald's happy meal within the M25. The brief was tough but this was extraordinary.

We did have quite a few problems casting *Beauty and the Beast* because the child, Chip, had to be a boy aged about 8 and under 4' 2". The young actors that played the part had regular measuring sessions in the company office because if they grew too tall the illusions did not work. We had a brainstorming session about how to raise awareness of the constant search for small boys and I came up with the idea of putting posters up by the ladies' toilets at the theatre because that is where women spend a lot of time queuing and so they would have plenty of time to read them. The posters announced that we were always 'Fishing for Chips' and to contact Jo Hawes if interested. I was very famous in ladies' toilets at the Dominion for some time. One of those posters is now in my own loo at home!

At the other end of the scale the open auditions for the London premiere of *Mary Poppins* attracted 1500 children to the Prince Edward Theatre one cold, Saturday morning. Such a turnout is fantastic. The press were there and I was hoping for a piece in the *Evening Standard,* which is always a welcome boost to the box office. Seeing so many children is essential for a show which requires exceptionally talented young actors. Parents and children were queuing round the block and the end of the queue met the beginning. It wasn't long before this attracted the attention of the police who strode into the foyer of the theatre asking who was in charge. They pointed out that children were queuing in the road and it was dangerous. Not wanting negative publicity my staff registered every child in double quick time and the queue was gone in an hour!

I have cast many children around the country for *Miss Saigon.* 'Tam' is a boy but often played by a 4 or 5-year-old girl. Boys of that age are generally not as mature as girls and they also have to look South-East Asian so it is always a challenge to cast it successfully. We always cast more children than we needed knowing that we would probably lose some of them in rehearsal. Being in a huge production like that is really intimidating for a tiny child.

I recall having to tell one particular Tam's parents that we would not be able to continue with him – he was 4 years old. A few days later I dropped my toddler off at his nursery school to be greeted by a very harrassed leader in the middle of a Christmas nativity rehearsal. I told her what I had been forced to do and she looked me straight in the eye and said 'Well, at least you can!'

13

Recalls

Recalls, sometimes referred to as call backs, are usual for roles in the theatre and there may be several before decisions are made. Sometimes children are told straightaway if they have been lucky enough to get a recall. I nearly always hand out letters so that all the details can be immediately given to mum or dad. Recalls may be on the same day or days or even weeks later. Parents and children should not leave the waiting room unless absolutely certain that it is alright to do so. There may be more than one recall spread over several weeks. Parents and children should try to take each audition as it comes and not look too far ahead.

The children, or more often their parents, are sometimes inclined to view the fact that their child has not been recalled as a sign of a lack of talent or as some sort of failure. Without a doubt some children come to auditions who should not be considering a career in the performing arts – this is true of adults too. However sometimes not being recalled, or even cast, might be nothing to do with talent. Occasionally it is absolutely clear from the moment that the child enters the room that the production is not right for them and it might be because they simply do not fit the basic criteria required for that particular piece.

THE ODDS!

Parents and children should resist the temptation to work out the odds of being offered a part because it is a pointless exercise. If, having been through the casting process we do not find the children we need, we start again.

In order to cast any part we must see a lot of children. On a new, high-profile show it is not unusual to see 1000 children in order to cast a few parts. We usually see fewer boys than girls. The ratio is roughly one third boys to two thirds girls. That is not our choice – it is simply that more girls attend classes and show an interest in performing than boys. This can often cause problems, especially on a show like *Oliver!* where there are a number of parts for boys who can sing, dance and act and each of those parts is shared by three children.

All shows have their particular problems and issues with casting, but clearly it is easier to cast a 10-year-old girl who dances beautifully and sings like an angel than a 14-year-old boy, under five feet tall whose voice has not broken!

FURTHER AUDITIONS

Sometimes there could be a number of recalls so take it one step at a time and keep a sense of proportion! Whatever happens the children are gaining valuable experience at each recall. It is not easy for the team either who are getting to know the children better and better through this process.

SCHOOLS FOR TRAINING CHILDREN FOR PARTICULAR PARTS

Some productions do not audition for children to go straight into the show but run weekly workshops instead. They train the children for a few months and then cast the parts from there. In a show that has particular challenges this is such a good way to make sure the production always has children ready to play the parts. It is a fabulous opportunity for the children who receive very high-quality training from the resident team attached to the show. Whether they make it into the show or not, they cannot fail to benefit from the classes which cost their parents nothing.

FINAL CASTING

These auditions make me nervous. Not casting enough children and having to start again is a bit depressing when so much hard work has gone into preparing the children for the finals and especially if we think we have a lovely selection of children to present. They are often attended by directors and producers who will not have attended before and will not know the children as we do. So if a child is having an off day it is hard, knowing them as we do at that stage, that they can do better. However, that is the system so we have to work within it and hope for the best.

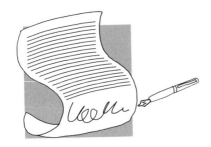

14

The Offer

Having attended a number of recalls, lived and breathed the show for several weeks or months, then comes the best part of all, the offer! After all the stress and tension, travelling backwards and forwards to the audition, waiting, worrying, hoping that it has all been worth it, now is the time to celebrate.

Parents react differently when I ring with such news. Some are so laid back I wonder if they really want the job for their child at all. Some are so excited I can hardly get a word out of them and some thrust the receiver into the hands of the screaming child who cannot speak either! I do not try to give any further information at this stage as whatever I say will usually go in one ear and out of the other!

Parents often thank me for giving their child the opportunity to be in a production and whilst this is very flattering I consider it misplaced to accept such thanks. The children create the opportunity for themselves by training hard and doing well in the auditions. No one can do that for them except themselves. All I can do is make the process as smooth as possible and if I achieve that then it is a job well done.

Sometimes, once the initial euphoria has worn off, parents are faced with the harsh reality that they have been less than honest with us and their child is not available for the whole period. The motive for this is obvious. They think that once their child is offered the part we will work round their various commitments. As I have already explained, honesty from the start about availability is essential. It is too late to explain after the offer that they are really sorry, that they are having sleepless nights and that they have only just realised that there is a clash and they are mortified that they could have allowed something like this to happen.

Assuming all offers are accepted I start the licencing process in time for the children to start rehearsals. I always hope that we have cast soon enough for me to do that comfortably.

PRESS/PUBLICITY

Productions usually have a carefully managed publicity machine and all press should be approved by the management. Any approach by the press directly to parents must be passed through the press representative and even if any journalist says that they have already spoken to the producer, parents should check. Sometimes the press are quite adept at letting parents think that they have been authorised to ask questions when they haven't but producers do like to keep a grip on publicity especially where children are involved. If such publicity is permitted, parents must try keep it in perspective. Today's news is tomorrow's fish and chip paper as they say.

One mother caused quite a stir on one of my shows by turning up unannounced at the stage door with a camera crew who were expecting to be allowed to film her child backstage. Needless to say they were unceremoniously turned away – I imagine it was extremely embarrassing for her!

AFTER THE AUDITIONS

Feedback after an audition is very rare. I am often emailed asking for feedback which I refuse to give for a number of reasons. It can be quite destructive since what is wrong for one show might be just right for another. It is also extremely time consuming and after a session of auditions in which perhaps 600 children may have been seen, to give feedback is simply not practical.

My advice to auditionees is this. Attend the audition as well prepared as possible. Do as well as possible whilst in the room, learn from the experience and forget all about it until or unless you hear an outcome.

Sitting by the telephone, the letter box or the email is not going to make the decision come any faster or even at all so look ahead to the next audition instead.

15

Licensing

fter the offer is made and accepted it is time to start the licensing process. This is really important and quite often urgent.

Licencing is complicated and detailed and I ask that when I send out the paperwork to parents they attend to it straight away. There are guidelines specifying the amount of time that authorities can insist they have in order to process a licence. It is most unhelpful if parents stick the paperwork under the bread bin and ignore it until I ring to find out if it is in the post yet. These parents are usually the same ones that are furious if their child is not allowed to rehearse because the licence has not been granted. The worst part of all this is that quite apart from the inconvenience to the production, the person most affected by such a lack of awareness of the importance of the licence is also the person who can do absolutely nothing about it, the child. This is unfair and although parents will give me all sorts of apparently valid reasons for not being able to return it all to me quickly, I am completely mystified as to why the majority manage to send it back very promptly while others take weeks. I will admit though that schools and doctors do vary in how quickly they produce their letters.

CHILDREN AND YOUNG PERSONS ACT 1963 – A CRASH COURSE

No child under school leaving age (which is 16 but defined by a date in June each year) can perform without a licence which is applied for by the producer's office, the applicant, and granted by the local authority in which the child resides (not where he or she goes to school which might be different).

In order for a licence to be granted the following paperwork has to be sent to the authority prior to the first rehearsal or performance. Education Authorities differ on this, as they do on many things:

- A form known as a **Part 1** fully completed and signed by a representative of the producer

- A form known as a **Part 2** fully completed and signed by the parent

- A photocopy of the child's birth certificate

- Two recent, identical, named passport-sized photographs

- A letter from the child's school stating that they support participation in the production. If a child is home educated then the parent should confirm this in writing but it makes no difference. The licence still has to be applied for in the same way as it would for a child educated at a school. If the licence is going to run across a change of school both schools must supply letters. Sometimes it is a challenge to obtain such letters if it is school holidays so an excellent relationship with the headteacher is helpful so that he or she can be contacted if necessary. If the job is happening entirely in school holidays a letter is not required but otherwise the licence will not be granted without school consent.

- Any relevant schedules or hotels if touring and any other information which must be supplied by the producer.

- A medical certificate or letter from a GP or other medically qualified person stating that the child is fit to perform. It must be dated as they only last for six months. Many doctors dislike having to do these but they are part of the legislation and, although there is a possibility they will be scrapped in favour of a parents health questionnaire, they are, at the time of writing, compulsory. Doctors usually charge for them which could be up to £65 or more. Some doctors will insist on doing a full medical, which is not required, while others will not even see the child but simply do a letter from the notes. Occasionally a doctor will insist on speaking to me before they do the letter and will tell me that they can only do a note based on what the child is like today. I have every sympathy but I still have to have it!

- If a child breaks a bone or has an infectious disease during a run I always insist on a new medical letter prior to their returning. Otherwise the producer may not be covered for insurance purposes. It is also a way of ensuring that the child really is fit to return as children are often desperate to come back sooner than they should, aided and abetted by their parents in some cases! We have to be sure.

THE RULES AND REGULATIONS (IN BRIEF)

- Children must attend fifteen hours of schooling a week as a minimum whilst working. This may be at their own school or with a private tutor. There is more flexibility if they are home educated of course but only because home education does not have the same degree of supervision as traditional schooling.

- Children can work for 3.5 hours, for a performance or rehearsal followed by a 1.5 hour break, and then another 3.5 hours for another performance or rehearsal.

- Children can only be licenced for one six month period at a time. Some authorities include rehearsal in this while others do not.

- Children can never work three sessions a day i.e. morning, afternoon and evening. They also cannot be called morning and evening on the same day since this counts as a three session day even if they are not working in the afternoon.

- Children must not come into the theatre or rehearsal room for a rehearsal or performance before 10am.

- Children are not supposed to be in the theatre after 10pm up to the age of 13 or 10.30pm if aged over 13. They can work until 11pm on eight days in any four weeks or three days in any one week, which is why I always recommend having three teams.

- Licence applications must be submitted to the authority 21 days before the child is due to start performing or rehearsing. However, since they have to be absent from school during rehearsal the local authority has to give permission for rehearsals. For this reason it is best to get all the paperwork to the authority three weeks before rehearsals start in case they refuse for whatever reason. Some authorities will grant licences quicker than this but it is at their own discretion.

- Children must be chaperoned at all times and boys and girls must be chaperoned separately on a one chaperone to twelve children basis. They must have a dressing room for each sex and separate toilet facilities from the rest of the cast. A reasonably sized dressing room can be divided in half by a partition of some sort. They are supposed to have natural light in the room but some of our theatres are not built to provide that. The inspecting authority (i.e. the authority in which the theatre is located) will inspect the dressing rooms and the facilities on behalf of each child's authority. They can inspect whenever they like and may not give warning.

- Authorities interpret the rules differently and may impose conditions in the licence. They may also revoke the licence with no notice if they think there is reason to do so.

- If there is a camera present children must finish performing by 7pm. They can film until 7.30pm in exceptional circumstances and this is at the discretion of the chaperone on the day.

- This Act of Parliament is currently under review and some changes are likely.

- Children no longer require a licence when they have reached school leaving age.

- The Children and Young Persons Act was passed many years ago and does not really fit the demands of the modern entertainment industry. One major problem is the differences in the laws surrounding the time children have to finish working in broadcasting and theatre. On the BBC's *I'd Do Anything*, which searched for Nancy and a boy to play Oliver, this caused many problems. The children were auditioning each week for a show which would finish at Drury Lane at 10.10pm but they are prohibited from filming after 7pm. Since the TV show was transmitted between 7pm and 8pm the children were required to film in advance and then sit in the studio in costume watching their footage on a screen. The results show was transmitted the next day and looked as if it was live when in fact it was all completed during the week and on Saturday afternoon in front of a live audience. I had several phone calls on Monday mornings from local authorities asking me why the boys were filming after 7pm on Saturday and why were they filming on a Sunday when they were not licenced to be there on that day at all. It took some patience to explain that the wonders of modern technology allowed the BBC to make everything appear to be live!

WORKING ABROAD

- **City of Westminster Magistrates' Court**
  If children are working abroad they are required to be licenced, not by their own local authority, but by City of Westminster Magistrates' Court. There is a lot of paperwork involved and the applicant is required to attend the court and appear in front of a judge to answer questions on oath. The applicant also has to send an application to the local Chief of Police in the borough in which the child lives. The hearing for licence applications is done at the start of the business day (10.30am) and whilst the applicant is being cross-examined lawyers, clerks of the court and indeed the first defendant are gathering in the court for the first case. This is usually a

thoroughly intimidating experience! However, recently I had to wait for a long time because there was a mix up with the paperwork. I sat in the courtroom for over an hour and eventually the Clerk of the Court called me into chambers to meet the judge. They had decided that he would sign the paperwork there. He was very businesslike in court, as is right and proper, so I was a bit apprehensive. Imagine my surprise when he greeted me with a beaming smile and asked me if I would like him to sing 'The Hills are Alive'!

- Children who work abroad sometimes have to be licenced in the other country as well as by the Court. It is often extremely tricky to satisfy both countries! In France, for example, there is a lot of paperwork to be done and the French legislation is not entirely compatible with the UK law – in fact much of it is a direct contradiction! I licenced children to perform in *Les Misérables* at the Chatâlet and this was certainly a very steep learning curve. Since it took me a long time to completely understand the various intricacies of the UK law I was very nervous about licencing in a foreign language. Whilst picking my way through this minefield it was so helpful to be able to translate everything on the internet including the application forms which I completed in English and then translated back into French! The licences in France are granted by committee and they only sit twice a month so there is no room for manoeuvre.

- If UK children are performing abroad where they do not require a local licence then they are required to abide by UK law just as if they were performing in the UK.

- Children coming in from abroad are required to be licenced by this country and abide by our rules including being chaperoned by a UK chaperone. They will not have a UK address so they will be licenced by the borough in which the producer's office is situated. This is not as straightforward as it seems, particularly because it does not happen that often so can cause much scratching of heads. The incoming company also may have their own way of doing things and do not necessarily like to have our rules and regulations imposed upon them. I discovered this when I was working on the all-Indian production of *A Midsummer Night's Dream* which toured the UK. It was a fabulous production but the cast could not understand why they had to abide by our rules and objected most strongly. The two children could not even speak English when they first came although the chaperone, Jon, worked hard to change that and they went home quite accomplished. The inspecting authorities took great exception to the fact that the boys, who had a circus background and were very skilled, were doing aerial acrobatics without harnesses or even a crash mat. They insisted that they should not be allowed to be higher than three feet off the stage and a crash mat was installed.

16

Breaching the Law

The law within which we all have to work is complicated and not entirely user friendly. However, it is there for very good reasons – the protection of vulnerable young people. Parents must realise that failure to comply with it has far-reaching implications that may not just affect the child. The penalties for breaching the law can range from a phone call from the LA to prosecution and a fine or three months in prison. Future licences may be affected. Parents who are willing to break the law forget that they may be jeopardising the licences of the chaperones or indeed the good name of the producer. It is important to attend school whenever possible for example. Children should not miss school to be well enough to perform or rehearse. My own son was recently rehearsing a show and questioned the point of going to school for just an hour and a half prior to a rehearsal when he was 'only' doing PE. I said that even if he was sitting looking at the wall for 90 minutes, that tick in the register is all important!

Unfortunately, parents are sometimes quite happy to allow their children to work in a way that is incompatible with the law, which is a good reason for not allowing them to chaperone. I was involved in a production some years ago which was scheduled to do a midnight matinee. As I have already said children cannot work in theatre after 11pm and this show was not even due to start until 11.30pm. The producer insisted that I ask each authority and, as I knew would be the case, they all said 'no way!' However the parents intervened in and let it be known that they would be quite happy for their children to take part. I had to explain to all parties that it didn't matter what the parents would or would not allow, the law was the law and this performance could not go ahead with children.

UNLICENCED WORK

Generally speaking performing children always require a licence. They can work for four days in a twelve month period unlicensed if:

- They have not worked in the preceding six months

- They are not missing school

- They are not paid

If children fit those conditions then they can work without a licence. If, however, all of the conditions do not apply then the employment is illegal and both the parent and the employer risk prosecution by the local authority.

MODELLING

Modelling should be vigorously regulated for licencing. Many photographic shoots are set up with hardly any notice and licencing is not even considered. This is a shocking state of affairs because what people do not realise is that an unlicenced child is also an uninsured child. Inspections do not take place because even if the LA finds out about the work, by the time they arrive it will all be over – these things happen really quickly. If parents and indeed agencies refused to cooperate with the big companies that use unlicensed children for modelling they would soon realise that the only way to use children is to become more organised and build in a longer lead time before the shoot.

LICENCING AT SHORT NOTICE

I have taken on a number of productions at short notice usually because producers do not realise that, unlike adults who can be cast today and start rehearsing tomorrow, it is much more complicated with children. Whenever I am asked when I would like to start casting I always say that it should be done sooner rather than later. On more than one occasion I have been telephoned to help out a production that has got into difficulties with the children and they need to do first rounds tomorrow, recalls the day after and the children are required to rehearse the day after that. This is a challenge to say the least, although it is possible and I have done it a few times.

17

Types of Theatre Productions

LONG-RUNNING SHOWS

These are quite common in the West End these days and they must be recast twice a year or so. Sometimes they are harder to cast than a new show because any new production is likely to be the one in which children are interested. Even so long-running productions must be recast as successfully every time as they were when they first opened.

WORKSHOPS

Sometimes a production may be cast, not for a full-scale production in a theatre but for a workshop. This is quite a common occurrence for a new show and will be a serious working session for the creative team and could take anything from a few days to a few weeks. At the end there will be one or two performances which will be given to an invited audience of people closely involved in the potential production, such as producers, backers, designers and so on. It will not be for the general public and parents are unlikely to be invited. The performers in the workshop may not be the ones who end up doing the show either but nevertheless these performances are an exciting event to be part of since they are a very creative process.

REHEARSED READING

Sometimes a play or musical, when it has been written or rewritten, will be read by a cast brought together by the director for the specific intention of seeing if it will work as a full-scale production. Again the performers may not be the cast chosen to do the production itself. This process will probably only take a day or two.

FESTIVALS

Many children are entered into their local festivals by their dance schools in various categories including singing, dancing and acting. They give the children valuable performing experience but there the similarity to professional work ends. I have had a lot of experience of pushy parents but these parents are in a class of their own! Children wear tons of make-up which is in direct contrast to the way they should arrive for auditions. Their parents also spend small fortunes on costumes and are ambitious for their children beyond belief. The children often receive gold, silver and bronze medals but such events rarely display talent that is comparable with the demands of professional performances. Parents sometimes become confused as to why a child who has won a gold medal in a festival does not even receive a recall when auditioning professionally. The techniques are entirely different and my experience of festivals is that many children are directed in the old school commonly known as 'eyes and teeth'. Professional productions, films and television dramas require very natural children these days and I can usually spot a 'festival' child a mile off.

Medals at festivals are granted on the basis of the best on the day, which unfortunately might not be terribly good. Recalls or offers for professional productions are made to the best children that can be found – sometimes this is over a long period of time. This is a very important difference.

I am not suggesting that if the opportunity arrives children should not take part but I do think it is important that the distinction is clear between festivals and professional auditions/performances.

18

Rehearsals

F or West End shows rehearsal will take about five weeks in a London rehearsal space. There are not too many venues around London that can cater for a large-scale musical which typically requires two large rooms plus one or two smaller spaces (for singing and fittings), a company office and possibly a tutor room. These venues are booked well in advance.

Children come into contact with many people when they are in a show: directors, choreographers, musicians, actors, chaperones, sound operators, stage management, wardrobe, wigs, crew – the list is extensive and all bring their particular talents to the production. For me it is part of the excitement that so many people with such diverse talents come together to create the show.

The company manager, in particular, is very important to the entire company and in charge of the whole show in the theatre and rehearsal room. Where children are involved it is important that it is someone who really understands children and can empathize with them. It is not easy to have children in a company and it does bring special challenges, especially on tour, where the company manager is often needed to give support to the chaperones.

Sometimes fittings take place before rehearsals start – they are an exciting part of the process and it is important that such appointments are kept. Costume makers come from far and wide and usually make a special trip to fit several cast members on the same day. If parents cancel at the last minute or simply do not turn up, it can be costly to the production and can cause delays in the costume being ready. A chaperone or parent should be present at children's fittings.

COACHING

Sometimes a script is sent out in advance and whilst it is excellent if it is learnt by heart (described as being 'off the book') as with auditions, children should not to be coached in how to deliver the lines. This is the exclusive job of the director and it is quite possible for parents to coach a child out of the part. Sometimes after a parent has watched a performance the child will deliver a completely different performance. This is exasperating for a team of professionals who know exactly how they want the piece to be performed. Having parents, teachers and grandma all chipping in with their opinion is so confusing for a child and can cause all sorts of untold problems. Restrict any comments to high praise!

I have on several occasions had to ask parents not to sit in the front row every night and then give their child notes. Leave it to the director to direct – not doing so can, in extreme circumstances, cost the child the job. This has happened to me once where a talented child was so confused by the conflicting notes he was being given by the director and his mother, that his performance fell apart despite the best efforts of everyone to help him. Sadly when it came to deciding whether he should stay on for a second contract, he was not asked to continue.

Rehearsals usually start with a 'meet and greet' – this is a chance for the producers, general managers, creative team, cast and crew to chat in the rehearsal room prior to the more formal proceedings. The producer and/or director will perhaps make an introductory or welcome speech and then everyone will introduce themselves. Typically this means everyone standing or sitting in a big circle and saying their name and their part or job. Sometimes this can be quite funny as some will crack a joke in the process. It is a great icebreaker!

At the first day of *Cat on a Hot Tin Roof* the director began by introducing herself and asked everyone to do the same and also to give their age. The first person to introduce himself was a child, Ben, aged 4. The children carried on round the circle and I could see the adults, especially the women, trying to decide whether they were also going to give their ages, refuse to do so or perhaps lie! The first adult after the children had introduced themselves had no such qualms and he promptly announced that he was 'James Earl Jones, aged 78'!

Following the introductions there is often a talk about the set given by the director and/or designer. They will use the model to take the assembled company through the show scene by scene, which is usually the first time most people will have seen it. By now it is probably lunchtime and afterwards there might be a read/sing through. Then the hard work begins, the actors, stage management and directors stay and most of the rest of the assembled crowd go back to their offices.

This period is a busy time in the theatre too as the 'get in' will be going on and will probably have already started. This is when the set is installed along with the lighting, sound and all technical equipment – in America this is referred to as the 'load in' or 'bump in'.

Towards the end of the rehearsal period the show is run with props but no costumes and the final run through takes place just before everyone moves to the theatre. This is attended by many of the personnel working on the show but who are not in the rehearsal room every day.

On the first day in the theatre, immediately before the technical period begins, the children and adults will be taken round the set with Health and Safety Issues in mind.

Technical rehearsals are the most difficult part of the whole period of any child's involvement in a production for parents because of their unpredictability. At this point the schedule will change hourly on occasions, tempers will be frayed, children will be called and not used and parents wonder why on earth they ever became involved in what they perceive to be a disorganised shambles. The difficulty with technical rehearsals is that nobody knows what is going to be done tomorrow until we reach the end of today. This is a short period in the life of the show and once performances start the production will settle down into a lovely routine. Parents should try to look past this very tricky period, which is usually only 10 days or so.

For me the technical period is the most exciting part – it is when the show really starts coming together and it might be painfully slow – sometimes it could take all day to tech five minutes of the show – but it is thrilling and frustrating all at once. Where there are two or three teams of children inevitably some will sit in the auditorium with a chaperone, watching while some are on stage rehearsing. Children may come home and announce that they have done absolutely nothing all day! This is not correct because they should have been paying attention to what was going on onstage so that they are prepared when it is their turn.

For the director and other members of the creative team, technicals involving children are very difficult. There are so many things that have to be done that rehearsing three sets of children simultaneously is often very challenging because time is so precious. Time runs away and we all have to carefully monitor what is going on so that we can be sure that all the teams are going to open successfully within a few days of the first preview. Otherwise the rules and regulations mean that we will soon run out of children.

During the technical period there will be half a day when the cast and orchestra meet for the first time. This is called the Sitzprobe. The band calls take place under the supervision of the musical director in a room away from the cast rehearsals. For a few hours at the Sitzprobe everyone comes together without set, costumes or staging. It is one of the most important and exciting parts of the entire process. Suddenly the show comes alive!

After the technical rehearsals are over the dress rehearsals start and it is ideal if there are enough so the teams can perform in one each. Sometimes the final dress rehearsal will be 'open' and this means that it will play to an invited audience. This will not be a full house – maybe only a couple of hundred people – and the show may stop once or even more. By this time the cast and crew have arrived at the point where they need an audience and, because the invited audience will be largely made up of friends and family, it will be supportive and encouraging – even riotous on occasions!

19

Performances

It is astonishing how everything comes together, although occasionally early previews are cancelled if there is no alternative and the technical rehearsals have been delayed due to problems of one sort or another. As a Stage Manager, I worked on a huge production called *Forty Glorious Years* which took place at Earls Court 2 and was mounted to celebrate the Queen's forty years on the throne. There were so many performers and performances taking part including Cliff Richard, a recording of *The Archers*, the military, horses, choirs, cars through the ages, short sequences from shows – it was absolutely massive. The whole thing only had eight days in which to rehearse in the venue and it was never run from beginning to end without stopping. There is no possibility of delaying when the Queen is coming so she unknowingly witnessed a dress rehearsal because that was the first time we had run it! Such occasions are thrilling and stressful at the same time because the show cannot stop when such an important audience is present.

Preview performances take place prior to the press being invited and can vary from a few days to several weeks. Ticket prices are often slightly lower than for performances after press night and during this period there are often rehearsals and many changes take place while the show settles down. Sometimes these changes can be quite dramatic, songs may be cut or added and by the first night the show might look very different from the way it was at the first preview.

PRESS NIGHT

As I have previously mentioned parents are often very competitive over the choice of which child or team performs on the press night and sometimes bitter rivalry takes place at the Stage Door. Interestingly the children are not as bothered as their parents. I have taken many phone calls from parents explaining to me why their child should have been chosen to do the press night. The truth is that someone has to do the press night and getting in a state about it is not going to change anything. Much better to relax and concentrate on the fact that all the children must be good or they wouldn't be there at all. It is not possible to please all of the people all of the time and we cannot have more than one team on the stage for any one night! Each team will have their moment of glory and increasingly in London we are adopting the American system of having several press nights and an opening night. Sometimes there are also gala nights during previews which are for charity and are often attended by members of the Royal Family. We try to spread out the special performances amongst the teams if possible.

During the run it is common for celebrities and household names of one sort or another to attend performances and sometimes they ask if they can meet the children afterwards. Michael Jackson and Mark Lester met Oliver and the Artful Dodger one night, Julie Andrews attended a performance of *Mary Poppins* in aid of UNICEF and Samantha Cameron attended *Oliver!* in aid of Help the Heroes. The Prince of Wales attended a gala performance of *Shrek the Musical* in aid of his own charity, The Prince's Trust. Big shows do generate quite a lot of publicity for themselves and charities by collaborating in this way and it all adds to the excitement for the children.

On the opening night itself the show plays to an invited audience made up of the rich and famous, the producers, family and other guests of cast and crew, parents and all sorts of people connected to the production. It is invariably glamorous and hugely exciting for the children, especially if they are invited to the party afterwards. Press night parties take place after the show in a venue elsewhere and are invariably in the week. Children are not always invited, however, because as much as they are part of a wonderful show and probably should be able to enjoy the fun of a party along with the adults, such events are not always the place for children. Producers vary in their attitude towards children being invited. Tickets are always limited and so there is often a discussion about who will take responsibility for the child and whether parents should be invited with their children. What about the children who are not performing on press night – should they be invited too? How many tickets should the non-performing children be offered for the performance? The questions are endless and the answers not straightforward.

The day after the press night – the critics have their say! With luck they have liked the show and everyone looks forward to a long and successful run. Rarely, it doesn't matter what they say – the show has fantastic word of mouth and advance ticket sales are good. But this is not always so, and after all the hard work by everybody it is very disappointing if the show flops.

Almost as soon as the ink is dry on the reviews I start to think about recasting the children because they cannot perform for more than six months on one licence. They can be extended but all the paperwork must be redone.

ONCE THE SHOW HAS OPENED

After the press night the production falls into a routine. Children will perform to their schedule except in the case of illness where swaps are unavoidable.

Rehearsals will continue because the adult understudies must be rehearsed. Children will be called for some of these and the more integral they are to the show the more likely they are to be called. These rehearsals are not every day though, are likely to be in the afternoons and since theatre productions usually have three teams of children the rehearsals can be spread out between them.

Producers and directors do swap children around on occasions, particularly during previews. It is best to be very practical with your child if this situation arises and try not to make a big thing about it. That is easier said than done but once the decision has been made it is very unlikely to be changed so making a fuss is not really going to help. Usually the parents are more upset about it than the children and it is not unusual for bad feeling to be stirred up at the stage door.

I have been asked to do swaps by the director or producer many times and I can only say, 'Please don't shoot the messenger!' because I don't like swaps either. Such decisions come from a much higher authority than me. As odd as it may seem sometimes it is for the good of the child who is being swapped out because he or she simply may not be ready for an audience.

When buying tickets parents should not choose to sit in the auditorium so close to the stage that they can be seen by their offspring. Some parents seem to treat it like a school play where it is acceptable for them to wave to their children as they make their entrance, although even that makes me wince! This is so unprofessional and whooping and cheering in the front row, whilst it might be great fun for the child's family, is likely to annoy the adult actors and embarrass the child. Family members will be sitting with other members of the public who have paid a lot of money to watch the show in peace and who do not want to have their evening spoilt by the actions of inconsiderate parents. Parents are naturally as proud of their child as they can possibly be which is right and proper but there are other more appropriate ways of showing it. What might be acceptable behaviour in school is absolutely not in a professional environment. Children will be reprimanded by the resident team if they react to such behaviour and parents should remember that their offspring are now young professionals and are expected to behave as such.

Parents should be sensitive to their children when coming in to the theatre to watch or when other family members or friends attend. Some children find it very stressful when they know that they have people watching and are under enormous pressure to perform well. Sometimes they really cannot handle it and parents should consider the stress they unwittingly cause to their children. Sometimes it is better for parents not to tell them that they have people watching until afterwards.

Parents frequently send their children to perform when they are unwell simply because their friends are watching. The chaperones will soon spot a sick child and it is their responsibility to send the child home if they think they are not well. Really sensitive children will find they may develop vocal problems due to all these pressures and whilst it is usually in their minds it is still very difficult to deal with both for them and for us.

However, many children are completely unfazed by their loved ones watching it. It is a question of parents knowing their child.

TICKETS

Free tickets, known as comps, are at the Producer's discretion, and are rarely given. Access to house seats is more likely and these are top price tickets held by the producer for VIPs, cast members and others involved with the production. They are allocated on a first come first served basis and are usually limited to a pair or two per person. House seats are tracked and it is most important that once they have been allocated they are used legitimately and not, for example, sold on to a tout for profit as they will most certainly be traced back to the original purchaser.

Cheaper seats are usually only available through the box office so once your child has a schedule, book early. Do keep track of who amongst your many friends and family might have bought tickets in case the schedule is changed by the production. In such circumstances tickets can usually be exchanged for another night. However, producers will not normally refund tickets if a child is absent due to illness.

Tickets can only be exchanged if they have been bought through the house seat system or the box office. Tickets booked through agencies or touts cannot be exchanged. Be very careful about buying tickets from agencies and touts anyway because you will often find that they are very expensive and may have a poor view of the stage. If the production has been on for a while and is not doing so well the half-price ticket booth in Leicester Square is an excellent place to buy tickets. This is operated by The Society of London Theatre. Tickets will be sold at half price for performances on the day and they will be the best available. Tickets cannot be purchased in advance from the booth, over the phone or on the internet. People have to turn up and take their chance.

HAIRCUTS

Designers on professional productions rightly have strong feelings about the look of the physical production (this means the set, costumes etc.) and that includes the way hair is dressed. Hair is often used to conceal radio microphones and therefore some length is important, especially with girls who might need fringes. If the production is of a particular period, modern hair styles are inappropriate so it is very important to take notice of any guidance on that.

A child announced to the other children in a dressing room on a production in 1996 that he was going to have a short haircut. This despite the fact that hair had to be longish and scruffy in the show. This was two days before he was due to finish. He added that there was nothing Jo Hawes could do about it. He duly visited the barber, had a No. 1, and I sacked him. I have since had to suspend a few children for a period of time until hair has grown back to an acceptable length. Sometimes parents ask us not to cut their child's hair because he is closing soon and they want the period style to have a chance to grow out. The audience do not know that he is about to close and it is as important for his hair to be correctly styled on the last night as it is the first. Hair should be treated like costumes and all parents must remember that it is subject to design decisions.

If a long style is required and your child resembles a sheep, talk to the chaperones but do not take it upon yourself to have a haircut without checking. This is all part of the discipline of theatre and, whatever style is insisted upon, hair does grow.

Do check heads regularly for head lice too as wig and hair departments sometimes refuse to touch any child infected and insist they are sent home. Parents might think that this is an overreaction and I might be inclined to agree, but it is best to treat head lice the way you would treat a child with measles – isolate and treat immediately!

STEPPING UP/ STAYING ON

Sometimes there is an opportunity to move into other roles on a long-running show if there are suitable parts – *Oliver!* is a good example. At Drury Lane there were three different types of child actors in each performance. The 'Workhouse' Children only performed in the first fifteen minutes of the show and then went home – it looked spectacular to have fifty children on the stage. The 'Who Will Buy' children were in the whole show in a number of scenes but were not part of Fagin's gang. Oliver, Dodger and Fagin's Gang made up the remaining group. During each team's run we auditioned children who wished to be stepped up for the next contract. These auditions were separate from any others for 'new' children who we did not know. I think it is unnecessary to bring our performing children into first round auditions with all the attendant stresses and strains. We simply sprang these auditions on the children when they were in the theatre anyway so there was no time for them to be nervous. They were much more relaxed and the atmosphere was quite different since the resident team and the children already knew each other very well. It was thrilling to watch children progress as they gained in confidence, ability and experience. We stepped up a number of children during the life of the show at the Lane. My own son was cast in *Oliver!*, initially in the workhouse scene. He was completely inexperienced and it was thrilling for him and for us. It was his very first job and he was performing in a world famous show starring Rowan Atkinson at one of the most beautiful and famous theatres in the world. I felt that he was very lucky to have been given such an opportunity and a few months later he was offered a bigger part. I saw in him the way that children can grow and develop through their participation in such productions and his confidence improved so much. He always wanted to be in Fagin's gang but when that didn't happen after 15 months of being in *Oliver!* he chose to leave of his own accord, saying it was time to move on. The maturity he showed in making that decision was gained from his complete *Oliver!* experience and I was so proud of him.

COVERING FOR ILLNESS

As mentioned before, two or three teams of children will play on a rota in theatre for legal reasons and so that they can cover each other. They are required to be on standby at home to perform at short notice. Being unavailable is unfair to the other children playing the part and to the production which is dependent on having a full team of children at every performance. 'The Show Must Go On' is not just a cliché – children are expected to appear for scheduled performances or to cover for illness in spite of family ties, celebrations, the weather, football matches, hobbies and so on. It is a real nuisance for families if their child is called at short notice but it is what is expected and required whatever else is going on at home. This is harsh reality and often takes parents by surprise. Ours is one of the few professions where non-attendance at the place of work can be a disaster. It would be inconceivable to perform *Oliver!* without Oliver or *Matilda* without Matilda. In the entertainment industry we work when other people want to play. Working on public holidays, at weekends and at Christmas is completely normal for us. My husband has performed on more Boxing Days and New Year's Eves than I care to remember!

Roald Dahl's
THE MUSICAL

REASONS FOR MISSING PERFORMANCES

All children and adult performers have to miss performances due to illness at some point. It is a nuisance but unavoidable. No child should try to perform when they are unwell because they will only be sent home and at such a late stage it is very difficult to get in a replacement. Children should not miss school to be well enough to attend a rehearsal or performance either. It is implied in the law: no school – no show. Sending a child in with a temperature is nothing short of irresponsible because stage lighting will only make it worse. Parents must be sensible and give the management time to bring in a replacement from another team by phoning and discussing the situation early in the day. The fact that there may be friends or family watching should have no bearing on any decision about whether or not the child is well enough – no child should perform when unwell out of fairness to themselves and the entire paying audience.

Parents often telephone me to talk about the fact that their child is unwell and to ask whether I think they should come in or not. It is very difficult to tell over the telephone and it is not helpful for parents to hand the phone to the child with the instruction that they should sing to me. I don't think this is the best way to judge fitness to perform.

SATS

If children are taking SATS and indeed other compulsory school exams during their run the schedule does sometimes have to be altered to accommodate them. Parents should mention it as soon as possible so that everything can be swapped round with plenty of notice. Sometimes the licences are granted on the understanding that exams cannot be missed. Occasionally schools will allow children to sit the exams to accommodate the show, which is great, but if they will not there is no alternative but to organize swaps.

THE PITFALLS OF ACCEPTING TWO JOBS AT ONCE

Licencing laws do not permit children to work on two different projects on the same day. The commitment involved in being in theatre particularly and the possibility of being called in to cover on an unscheduled day means that accepting two jobs across the same period is bound to lead to trouble sooner or later. Long runs are tiring anyway and that combined with regular schooling is enough for any young person.

Twice I have experienced parents thinking they could have it all and in both cases the child was sacked from one or the other production. It is simply not worth the aggravation or the risk.

One morning I took a phone call from a parent who told me her child was unwell on a matinee day – it did not occur to me to ask any questions because I always assume I am being told the truth and so I duly replaced him. A couple of hours later I discovered he was actually in a show at another theatre that day and had arrived in the dressing room boasting about how he had gone sick from his other show! After several hours of wasted time, which I bitterly resented since none of this was of my doing, I uncovered a web of lies and deceit which resulted in the child being sacked from the other production and suspended by me from mine. The parents admitted to me that they wanted to 'have their cake and eat it.'

This was not the first time that this happened – on another occasion the parent asked me (once the dust had settled) whether it would affect their child's chances of being offered another part. Of course it will because it is a terrible way to treat any production. I cannot sit next to a team of directors and, faced with the same child, not mention to them what had happened before.

Children are not born knowing how to be professional. They look for guidance from adults and especially from their parents. When it all goes wrong who is it that is punished? Not the parent who condoned it but the child who has been ill-advised. An agent said to me once that it wasn't fair to punish the child for the actions of the parents. What am I supposed to do? I cannot suspend the parents however much I might like to. I would urge all parents to think carefully before they embark on such a risky course of action.

SALARY

In theatre children should receive half of the current adult Equity minimum divided by eight for performances. Equity minimums paid to adults are based on the size of the theatre in which the show is performing. Children are paid per performance, not per week because they do not do an eight-show week. Some producers do not pay children at all and whilst it is frowned upon not to pay it is up to parents to make a decision as to whether to accept the terms and conditions. Weigh up the experience the child might be getting if they do appear in a production unpaid. Children should be paid because if the show requires them then they should be remunerated accordingly. However, I can see that there are some circumstances in which it might be acceptable and these days even adults take unpaid work in order to get on the ladder. This is a contentious issue that has attracted much media comment.

Any salary will be paid to the child or to their agent so children must have their own bank account. Sometimes the licence will stipulate how much money must be saved for the child's future and when a subsequent licence is applied for authorities may ask to see the bank statement or savings book.

TRAVEL TO AND FROM REHEARSALS/ PERFORMANCES

It is stated in the Children and Young Persons Act that children should be accompanied on their journeys to and from the theatre, studio or rehearsal room at whatever time of day or night. Whilst they might travel to and from school unaccompanied, this is not permitted under the Act even with parental permission. Nor can anyone other than an adult collect them – this includes older siblings who might not have reached the age of 18.

This makes the commitment to parents even more onerous and is a big consideration particularly if there are younger siblings who must be cared for whilst a parent is collecting from a theatre at 10.30pm.

Travel is often an area of conflict with parents. Parents sometimes give permission for a child to go home with another parent who then walks round the corner only to release the child to travel in a different direction by himself. This may seem like a great way to buck the system. However, it does not take into account the fact that the person that has signed for the child has a legal obligation to see the child home. On the day the child has an accident, questions are asked and suddenly someone is in court. The question is – who? The chaperones have released the child in good faith and parents must understand that when children are working and under licence the rules are strict. The law clearly states that until they reach school leaving age they must be accompanied. I am often aghast at the cavalier way parents are with their children – it seems to me that they are our most precious asset and allowing them to disappear into the London Underground at 10.30pm by themselves is irresponsible to say the least.

At some point during every run a parent will test me on the travel issue and ring saying that it is too late for them to get there and they are sending a taxi or that the child has their permission to go home alone. It isn't for parents to give such permission. It is like allowing a passenger to travel in their car without a seat belt. It is illegal and their child's licence is in jeopardy and, very importantly, so is that of the chaperone whose livelihood is under threat. If the licence is taken away they might never work again. Also the licence holder, me, can be taken to court for breaching the regulations. So I will not allow children to travel home alone under any circumstances and my answer is always the same, 'You come – we'll wait'. They don't try it again.

Travelling to rehearsals or performances alone is also not permitted but it is often impossible for chaperones to know. Parents may drop off and run. Children cannot go through the stage door until the chaperones arrive, however, so if there is an accident while the child is waiting outside parents are still responsible.

20

Chaperones and Tutors

It is very easy to sit round a table interviewing men and women as chaperones but the real test is seeing them with the children. So I really prefer to employ people that I already know. For tours in particular I like to feel that if I am happy for my own children to go away with our chaperones then I am happy to send other people's children away with them. I feel the responsibility of selecting these people very keenly and like to choose them with the head chaperone and, if possible, the company manager, because they are the ones who are going to be working with them in the theatre on a daily basis.

When I am first approached about a show one of the things that crops up early on is how much the chaperones should be paid. My answer is nearly always the same, especially if it involves living in. They should be appropriately remunerated. I think chaperones do an extremely difficult job and I admire the men and women that do it and manage to keep their sense of humour. Chaperones have to know the law, they have to like children, have endless patience, understand this crazy business and often have to look after several noisy children for hours at a time. To supervise a number of exuberant children not related to you or to each other seems to me to be a job of immense difficulty. Add to this the sleep deprivation they encounter when on tour and they have to spend night after night trying to settle a number of hyperactive children, it is clear that this is no ordinary job.

Directors sometimes see chaperones, and probably myself, as a necessary evil who stop them working the children beyond permitted hours. They are often not appreciated by parents either whose sole intention seems to be to make the chaperones work very hard for their money and complain about absolutely everything! The parent who refuses to believe that their child could possibly be doing anything at all that might incur the chaperone's wrath is unrealistic about the ability of the child to behave differently from the way parents might expect, when they are in a pack.

Chaperones have a right to expect that parents collect their children punctually after a rehearsal or a show. This is particularly important after performances because the licence usually states by what time the children must leave, which is typically thirty minutes after curtain down. Sometimes parents are appallingly late and far from being apologetic they seem to think that it is the chaperone's job to wait around until they choose to arrive. This is unfair and, if for no other reason, children should be taken home as soon as possible so that they can sleep.

As with performing children, chaperone licences are granted by the local authority in which they live. They are required to be with the child(ren) all the time and to oversee their pastoral care. They must understand and know the clauses of the Children's Act that relate to theatre and be prepared to make sure the Act is respected.

I think that it is far too easy to obtain a chaperone's licence and I wish that there was more emphasis on training by all local authorities – only some of whom offer training. There should be a standard procedure that all authorities must follow. All chaperones must have an enhanced CRB and a licence but training is up to the discretion of the LA. The CRB itself is only as good as the day it was done and if parents have any real concerns about a chaperone they must not be afraid to say so.

If your child expresses concern about absolutely anything it is better to be safe than sorry.

People are inclined to think that chaperoning is an easy job and I often have letters or emails from newly licenced chaperones. Sometimes these are 'resting' actors and actresses and I rarely employ them because I prefer to employ experienced, career chaperones who really do understand what it is they are doing. My policy is not to employ parents as chaperones when their own child is in the show either. I think this is unfair to the child and to the other children also.

TUTORS

It is rare to employ tutors for London productions unless any children are from out of London and being accommodated by the production. In this case a school will be set up in the theatre and children will attend as if they were at their own school. The classes are likely to be tiny – maybe even one to one. However, producers avoid having to employ tutors if at all possible because it is very expensive.

On tour, if the children are local they will attend their own schools but if they are touring they must be tutored by qualified, CRB checked teachers. For primary school children it is relatively easy to find people to do this although they are an additional expense for the production. The teachers I employ might be supply teachers, in between jobs or perhaps recently retired. For secondary school children it is much harder because older children are taught by subject teachers. It is not possible to employ lots of different teachers so an acceptable compromise must be found.

Children should either always be with a chaperone or the chaperone will be able to see them on a monitor if they are onstage. They are never allowed to wander around the theatre by themselves. Theatres can be quite dangerous places and they must be treated with respect – they are not adventure playgrounds. Sometimes the children may find decisions which are made by the chaperones difficult to understand but chaperones will always have safety at the forefront of their minds. These days many sets use a lot of automation, scenery that moves around electronically, and the moving pieces are heavy. The children must realise that by not behaving as instructed by the chaperones they risk injury. It is a bit like standing on the pavement whilst a juggernaut is approaching. The child is told not to step into the road and they do so anyway. Such disobedience could have disastrous consequences on a moving set. If a child comes home complaining that the chaperones or stage management are strict in the wings parents should understand that there will be very good reasons.

All parents and children receive a copy of my anti-bullying policy on my shows so that everyone is aware that I operate a zero-tolerance attitude to bullying:

- Every child has the right to enjoy his or her work, free from intimidation both during the performances and in the breaks.

- We will not accept, and will question, any unkind actions or remarks, even if these were not intended to hurt.

- Any wounding action or comment will be called bullying and will be dealt with seriously.

- Everyone has a duty to report bullying which is too important to ignore.

It is a great shame that sometimes bullying does take place in the theatre during a production. It is always difficult to deal with and my heart sinks when I receive a phone call from a parent who thinks their child is being bullied. I will always follow up such a complaint but with an open mind because I am aware that neither myself nor the parent have actually heard or witnessed anything untoward. Additionally the 'bully' can be very clever and do their deeds subtly and out of sight of the chaperones. These days the mobile phone is often used for the purpose.

My preferred method is to listen to the parent who is making the complaint, consult with the chaperones and possibly other members of the team, and then talk to the parent of the bully. The initial phone call invariably has one of two responses. They either say 'It couldn't possibly be my child' or alternatively 'That's dreadful and I will speak to him or her about it immediately'. It is never easy to deal with and sometimes the best way would be to swap the teams around but that seems to me to punish the child in the other team just as much – they have done nothing wrong and are happy and settled only to be told that they must swap because someone else has stepped out of line.

Usually such situations are resolved after I have talked to both the children together and encouraged them to talk about their differences. It is often not as one-sided as it is first presented to me. The anti-bullying policy is quite clear and I encourage parents to talk to me about any problems before they become a very big issue. Parents are of the belief that I won't see their child for other productions if they make a fuss. This is misplaced anxiety because I just want all the children to have the time of their lives and since bullies usually operate in an air of secrecy and intimidation, the only way to deal with them is to flush them out.

Sometimes there is no alternative but to terminate the contract of a child on a production for artistic reasons or because of bad behaviour. This is a decision that is never taken lightly partly because the licencing process takes time and a production cannot limp along without the correct number of children for very long. The psychological effect on the child must be considered but sometimes we simply have no alternative.

A badly behaved child is a liability in theatre which is a place of work. It is often dangerous because of moving scenery and although all shows are carefully assessed for risk nothing is ever completely risk free. Bad behaviour also unsettles other children in the team and indeed encourages them to follow suit. The safety of the children and everyone around them is of paramount importance and there is a limit to the number of times warnings can be given only to be ignored. Unfortunately the majority of children that I have had to sack have been boys.

Occasionally a child simply cannot fulfil the role and this is deeply upsetting because the creative team sometimes feels some degree of responsibility. However in such circumstances it is unrealistic and cruel to continue to try to achieve the unachievable and not fair on the public either who have paid a lot of money to watch the performance.

This does sound as if I make a habit of sacking children! If we find that we have a situation in which one child is disrupting other children who in turn follow suit we do find that the only way to deal with it is to terminate the contract of the ringleader. This tends to bring the rest of the kids up short when they realise that losing their part is a very real possibility if they do not behave. However this is a last resort. Over the last 17 years and thousands of children that I have had in dozens of shows I have sacked only a handful. It is always unpleasant and must be the worst part of the job. However, sometimes it is unavoidable especially if the parent is unable to accept that children are inclined to behave differently when in a group. I rely on the parental support to avoid the worst happening.

For every child that I have been forced to release from a show there are many more who have gained so much from their involvement. Children who come from troubled backgrounds, in particular, find an escape and a release in their work and I know that in some cases their lives have been changed forever. I am extremely proud of these children because I know that some have unimaginable problems but still come in night after night and deliver a performance that gives no clue to the turmoil in their home lives. These are professional child actors and they are to be admired.

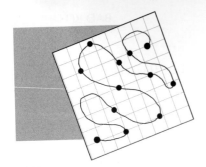

Touring shows which feature children both in the UK and abroad are a different kind of challenge. Touring children is very expensive – the cost of travelling, accommodation, chaperones, tutoring and food is immense. So if the show is going to be playing long enough in a large UK touring venue it is best to cast the show with children from the local area if it is at all possible. However this is not always practical if the show is only playing at a venue for a week or two and the children's parts are featured. They could rehearse for longer than they are performing so for those productions children must tour as part of the company with chaperones.

On a long tour this could mean six months but it does not mean that they will be away for all that time. Three teams of children can rotate quite happily and go home whenever they are not performing, working on a rota of a week on and two weeks off or three days on and six days off for example. It is vital that they retain strong links with home, school and their own friends. When children come into a show they have perhaps been through several rounds of auditions and physically it is a tough achievement. Mentally it is usually very easy to settle into the routine of a show on tour. The children are doing something they want to do and which they are good at and love.

Leaving a show is a different story. The children have lived in a very different world to many of their peers. They have experienced things most children do not experience and probably worked with household names. They are treated like adults and may have attracted press attention and critical success in their role. Sometimes it is difficult to adjust to normal life again and the more they are away the harder this may be. Keeping their feet on the ground is vital to ensuring that this readjustment is as smooth and successful as possible.

I am often surprised at the lack of questions that I am asked by parents when we are touring children, especially the younger ones. We make every effort to ensure that the children are as well looked after as possible. Chaperones, hotels and tutors are chosen with care and travel is arranged with meticulous attention to detail. I know this but the parents of newly cast children do not and I often think that I would certainly be asking more questions if I was in that position.

When children tour they usually stay in hotels, or possibly a flat, with chaperones and are tutored by qualified tutors. It is better for their education if they bring set work from their own schools so that they keep up with what their classmates are doing and do not fall behind. Sometimes the classes are so small that they whizz through the work and end up ahead of their peers, thus giving their head teacher no cause for complaint when the next job comes along! Children who attend private schools tend to have to work harder because we run our terms on state school dates which have shorter holidays.

Sometimes children are initially homesick on tour. The chaperones are very used to tears at bedtime and they do not usually last long. Parents can help by not telephoning late at night, however much they would love to say goodnight. When children are tired they are more likely to be upset if they hear Mummy or Daddy on the phone. Usually the child has unloaded their anxiety to the parent and then sleeps like a log leaving the poor unfortunate parent at home worrying about their baby all those miles away! Children share hotel rooms on tour because it is much better for them to be together in a twin or triple room than in single rooms. But this does mean that ringing at an unsociable hour is likely to wake everyone. The chaperones do not go to sleep until the children do so any delay has them pacing the corridor for hours!

During one tour a parent rang me after midnight and although I was up I did not answer, preferring to listen to the message as it was so late. She left a message berating me for the fact that I was obviously in bed while her child was still up and sobbing on the phone because she was homesick. What I was going to do about it? she asked. Once she had hung up I took a deep breath and rang back. I pointed out that I was not in bed but still working – listening to her message in fact, since I find that it is much better to call back straight away than wait until the morning.

The show was in the middle of technical rehearsals in the north of England at the time and this is the hardest time in any show whether it is on tour or in London. Tempers are frayed and schedules are changed at short notice. Parents usually shout at me at some point during this period on any production. I am happy to listen but I can rarely do anything about it.

I explained to the mother that the child had been in school during the morning and had then taken part in two rehearsals. She was bound to be tired so hearing mummy on the end of the phone was certainly going to provoke tears especially if she was in any way predisposed to homesickness.

This explanation did not calm her down at all. Sometimes only shock tactics will do. I said that since the technical rehearsals were nearly over this intensive working was almost at an end and so we had two choices. We could either go with it for a few days more by which time everything will have settled down, or she could collect her child from the venue the next day, take her home and I would recast the part.

She calmed down at once, assuring me that neither herself or her child would want to be released from the show at this stage.

No parent wants their child to leave a show once they have been through so much to be cast. The child does not want to leave either, which is more important to us because if the child were seriously unhappy then we would insist that they left the show for their welfare irrespective of what the parent might want. A sense of proportion in such situations on the part of parents is terribly important and phoning in the morning after a good night's sleep is probably a better idea than phoning last thing after a hard day.

Sometimes parents phone complaining that their child has not been in touch with them at all and asking whether they are all right. How brilliant! They are probably having a wonderful time and are simply too involved and busy to phone home. Whilst this might be off-putting for the parents I think it shows great maturity on the part of the child who may only be 7 years old.

Chaperones often confiscate mobiles at certain times during the day. This is to stop texting in class or photography and phone calls during the performance. It is not to prevent parents from having contact with their child. Recently we discovered cases where children carried two mobile phones, one to hand in and another to continue using whenever they think they can get away with it. I assume that parents are aware and condone this but it is not helpful.

The best way for parents and children to approach a tour is to imagine that it is similar to a spell at boarding school. Restrictions will apply but the children will have much more fun! As unpalatable as it might be to the parents, the children may not want to come home. Indeed for London shows I have occasionally asked the Sylvia Young Theatre School to accommodate a child who we have found to play a particular part but who lives too far away to commute. On more than one occasion these children have not returned to their own school but remained in London as a boarder well after their contract has ended! I have also known parents relocate their entire family to the London area so that they can support their child in their quest to be an actor.

LATE NIGHTS

Parents often worry about the impact late nights will have on their child, and although they do get tired they seem to thrive on it. It is the parents who are inconvenienced and this is understandable. In the West End or on tour children cannot work every night so if they are on a rota some of their late nights will be at the weekend when they can catch up the next day. Some schools will allow children to go in a bit late the next morning but my advice is to send children to school on time as much as possible. It is important to think about any future job and keeping the head teacher on your side is vital if permission is to be granted for a further licence.

Mealtimes will need to be adjusted to accommodate performances and parents must remember that children will only be allowed to eat certain things and drink water when they are in costume. This is to protect costumes from spillages – coloured fruit juice does not go well with a beautiful white costume and it could be disastrous if they are about to go onstage. Costumes are often extremely expensive and difficult to clean or replace and there are rarely spares available.

LEAVING THE SHOW

It would be brilliant if children are ready to leave when the time comes. They can enjoy a family holiday which they may not have had for several months. The reality is that children miss the show, their friends, the routine and the performing. Sometimes they miss it terribly and have trouble settling back down into the normal routine of school, family life, homework and so on. Parents can really help here and it starts when the child is still performing. Whenever they are scheduled off it is vital to keep them in their preshow routine so that it is not such a shock when the contract comes to an end.

A production can close with as little as two weeks' notice if it is no longer selling enough tickets at the box office. Sometimes this might be before the end of the child's contract. I have worked on a production that had its notice while children were still rehearsing and they didn't even open, which was very disappointing for them. This is very rare because it is expensive to audition and rehearse children so it is preferable if closure is planned with the children's schedule in mind.

Some children go from show to show and never stop working. This is unusual though and breaks in between jobs are good for the whole family!

23

Child Protection

PHOTOGRAPHY / WEBSITES

Photography, apart from the official production photographer, is generally prohibited in theatre for many reasons. There are often copyright issues to contend with and some celebrities do not like to be photographed when they are working. Facebook is increasingly a problem and whilst parents might be happy for their own child's photograph to be on the net there may be another child in his photograph whose parents may not feel the same. It is very important to monitor children's Facebook pages and to explain to them that trying to be 'friends' with adults puts them in an awkward position. There may be all sorts of things on an adult page that parents may not wish their child to see and the adult members of the company are usually advised by the management to refuse any requests from children to be friends. They are not intending to be unfriendly but they have to protect themselves from any accusations of inappropriate behaviour when they are working with children.

I have recently begun to insist that when children are cast in my shows they suspend their pages on internet sites for their own protection and to protect the production. I find many parents are relieved about this.

HEALTH AND SAFETY

All sets are inspected by Health and Safety and risk assessments are done to ensure that all precautions are taken to protect everyone working backstage, not just the children. The local authority in which the theatre is situated have a right to drop in unannounced to inspect at any time. I usually invite them in during the technical rehearsals especially if there is anything in particular that I am concerned about.

During an inspection they will check the licences, the well-being of the children, the chaperones and the dressing rooms. Nothing that affects the children is off limits, which is how it should be. In a show where the children might fly on a Kirby wire such as in *Peter Pan*, or sit on a roof in *Mary Poppins* and fly high above the stage in a car named *Chitty Chitty Bang Bang*, it is important that they are safe and protected. The *Mary Poppins* roof caused some concern in Bristol when we were inspected because it was so cleverly constructed that it looked much more dangerous from the auditorium than it actually was. As for Chitty – the children were quite safe and wore seat belts but I must say I was quite surprised how steeply it banked when I flew in it during the technical rehearsals.

On the recent tour of *Goodnight Mr Tom* there is a scene in William Beech's mother's house where the set closed down like a box whilst a child is lying on the floor underneath it. Once closed there is no room to do anything more than crawl to the exit even as a child. During the technical rehearsal in Chichester where it opened, one of the three boys playing William was very nervous about this particular scene and I was asked what I thought should be done. I said that I could not justify it to any LA who might phone me questioning it unless I had experienced it myself. So we had this hilarious half hour where all three boys playing William Beech, myself, the production manager and Heather Miller (our chaperone) all laid down flat on our stomachs while the set closed on top of us. We did it several times starting in full light and gradually getting to the point where the light was at its show level. All the boys were fine about it by the end of the rehearsal as was I. The director, Angus Jackson, had been quite happy to change the blocking if necessary but it was a very poignant moment in the play and I was pleased that it could be left as it was.

Sometimes something unexpected might happen days, weeks or even months after a show has opened which might provoke a change onstage. In *Beauty and the Beast* in London the child playing the role of Chip sat in a truck (a box on wheels) which formed the illusion that he was just a teacup as only his head was visible. The stage was on a rake (angled down towards the audience) and one night the truck set off by itself, with the child aboard, down to the orchestra pit and ended up with the child upside down suspended over the musicians. After that the truck was held by an actor to stop it moving!

Sometimes the number of chaperones on a show has little to do with the number of children performing. Whilst the ratio is recommended as 1.12 in the legislation, on the recent production of *Oliver!* at Drury

Lane we had ten chaperones for fifty children. This was entirely due to the enormity of the set and the fact that children appeared and disappeared through every conceivable entrance and exit!

Sadly I have been involved in a production where the first preview was so long (nearly four hours) that I had to take the child off before she had even made her entrance. As the show was new, we were unsure exactly what time she would be appearing, but the Education Authorities, knowing that I had a problem on my hands, gave me dispensation for a couple of weeks to keep the children there until 11pm. I did not feel I could leave the very difficult decision of taking the child off to the chaperones so I appeared at the theatre at 10pm to find one very excited little girl in her costume waiting to go on. Her parents were watching. At 10.50pm it was clear that we were not going to get to her entrance in time and I took the decision that she had to leave the theatre. She was so upset and eventually the show was shortened but it closed after a few weeks.

FAN MAIL

Children do sometimes receive fan mail which is sent to the stage door and these letters, however lovely they may seem, should be treated with caution. My chaperones do not allow members of the public to take photographs of the children when they are out and about with them for their safety, and I advise the parents to do the same. Unfortunately we live in a dangerous world and our children have a right to expect that we will protect them as far as we can. In a high-profile and visible environment such as theatre it is our responsibility, as adults, to be vigilant.

PHOTOGRAPHIC MEMORIES

Principal children will probably have a photo and short biography in the programme. Ensemble children may simply be listed or sometimes a group shot is taken. They are generally not available for purchase as the copyright belongs to the producer. Not all children will end up in the souvenir brochure because the photos are taken during a dress rehearsal and whichever children are performing then will be photographed. There is nothing sinister in that and although it is disappointing it happens on every show – there is no conscious decision about which children are photographed because the photographer will have been booked many weeks in advance in most cases. However, many parents are very upset that they have no photographic memories of their child's performance. Even so, they must not try to film or take photographs from the auditorium because it is likely to attract the attention of the theatre management to an embarrassing degree. Apart from the fact that such footage looks awful on Youtube which is where it often ends up, it is a criminal offence to film performances and the management have the right to delete images and can prosecute.

UNSUITABLE CONTENT

Sometimes the production that the children are in is not suitable viewing for a child and sometimes they are required to take part in a scene which is very unpleasant. In the latter case it is usually more distressing for the audience to watch, and especially the parents, than the children. During *Macbeth* Banquo's three children are murdered. In Rupert Goold's production at the Gielgud this was done in strobe lighting and one of the children apparently had her head sawn off. It was rehearsed very carefully in full light and the children had a good relationship with the actors so it really was no problem at all. The effect was amazing.

The Fix at the Donmar Warehouse was another example. The boy, Calvin Chandler Jr. appears right at the very end for about three minutes. The technical period was very long and slow and the three boys sharing the role were quite bored in the dressing room so we went into the auditorium to watch. We hadn't been there for many minutes when the leading actor (John Barrowman) looked up and said – 'This bit's not suitable, Jo'. So we beat a hasty retreat!

I always invite the LA into a rehearsal in such circumstances so that they can see that everything is being done by the book and tell me if they have any concerns. Sometimes audience members might write to the theatre, the producer or even the LA with their worries so I do like to be transparent and to feel that we have protected the children as much as is humanly possible.

DRESSING ROOMS/BACKSTAGE AREA

Parents, relatives and friends are not permitted backstage or in the rehearsal room. This is for very practical reasons. Theatres are often cramped backstage, and are a place of work. The more children appearing in a show (*Oliver!* for example, had fifty children in the show every night) the more parents there are who could potentially come backstage. The children are expected to behave like the professional performers they are and should be allowed to prepare for their performance in an appropriate way. Once they arrive for the performance, typically an hour or so prior to curtain up, they will be busy with warm-ups, getting into costume, hair and make-up has to be done and they will possibly be given notes on their performance by the resident team. The management are employing the child not the parent and it is reasonable that parents are treated in the same way as a relative of an adult performer.

During the show it is usually not possible for parents to wait anywhere in the theatre unless they are paying like any other member of the audience. This is often the most difficult part for parents. There is rarely time to go home and come back again unless they are lucky enough to live very close to the theatre. I sympathise but cannot really offer a solution. Sometimes parents offer to chaperone and I can understand the logic behind that but it is my policy not to employ parents as chaperones except in exceptional circumstances. I believe that chaperones should be professional, trained and independent of any family ties. That way it is easier to keep order and fairness.

I have in the past taken over productions that have transferred into the West End from a theatre outside London. Parents might already have been used as chaperones and despite the fact that I always want to bring in professional chaperones I am not always allowed to do so on an established production.

On one occasion I went into a theatre during technical rehearsals and discovered the children onstage and the parents, who were the chaperones, in the auditorium chatting. They had no idea what I was talking about when I suggested that they really ought to be backstage with their children. Local authorities can and do make spot checks and they can revoke licences if they think that the rules are not being followed. My chaperones are my eyes and ears in the theatre on a daily basis and I rely on them to make sure the law is kept. This includes the fact that children must <u>never</u> be left by themselves.

24

Superstitions and Ghosts

Theatre folk are very superstitious. Whistling in the dressing room, wishing someone good luck when break a leg is the accepted term and quoting the Scottish play are all likely to offend someone. Whilst some people may not be at all superstitious the children will come across others who are and they may insist that they do weird things to undo the perceived damage!

As an ASM ago I worked on a pantomime at the Theatre Royal Windsor where a member of the chorus, an adult, quoted from the Scottish play, which incidentally I never mention by name because I am very superstitious. He scoffed at the superstition surrounding it. During that particular performance a piece of scenery fell out of the flys and knocked him out. Coincidence? Who knows?

There are lots of reported sightings of theatre ghosts. If a child comes home telling his parent tales of the supernatural don't dismiss it as poppycock. I completely believe there are ghosts in theatres – my husband definitely saw one at the Palace Theatre in Shaftesbury Avenue during the run of *Les Misérables*. He was approaching the gent's toilet under the stage in the interval and clearly saw someone enter before him. Once inside, the toilets were completely empty.

I also recently heard a lovely story about sightings at the Palace Theatre in Shaftesbury Avenue during the renovation of the box office. The builders had seen a man walking around both front of house and on the stage wearing a top hat and tails. No one seemed to know who he was but the builders assumed he was an actor. Later some ancient photographs were discovered and leaning against the original box office was the same man – Charles Morton – wearing top hat and tails! He was the Theatre Manager in the 1800s.

During *The Pirates of Penzance* at the Theatre Royal Drury Lane two musicians went in to the theatre late at night to collect some instruments (I am assured they were perfectly sober!). A bed was being stored upstage which was nothing to do with the show and they both saw a man lying on it who winked at them as they walked past. Ghostly sightings are numerous and for me it is a fascinating part of theatre life.

25

Reflections from Children
and their Parents

On auditions	Fun!
	I was desperate to audition.
	Definitely nerve-wracking
On being offered a part	Thrilled – I didn't think it was real
	I was excited that my first job was *Oliver!*
	It was pretty big!
On rehearsal	Rehearsals were the best bit.
	It is hard work but you learn so much.
	Rehearsals were great, but very tiring!
On technical rehearsals	Boring! But it is the first time for everyone so I didn't want to moan.
Press Night	So frightening but the party was amazing!
	The party was really cool, and me and my friends were able to meet some celebrities.
On Leaving	I was so upset on the last night.
	Everyone was crying.
	Afterwards I was bored and I really missed it. I felt it was time to go though as I had been in the show 15 months. I made lots of friends.
	Being a part of *Oliver!* was an absolutely amazing experience and I loved every minute of it!

I am including here the thoughts and recollections of a few children – some now grown up, and parents who have been through the tremendous experience of being involved in West End shows. I include these so that these real experiences can encourage and reassure any parent whose child is begging to be allowed to audition for something and I hope it will prove that it really is an unforgettable experience.

Ros Duncombe, the parent of an *Oliver!* workhouse child who later moved into a bigger part. Her daughter had never performed before. The workhouse children were only in the first fifteen minutes of the show, were all cast from a town in the M4 corridor and travelled backwards and forwards to London on a coach provided by the production. The parents and children were extremely inexperienced.

'Having been shown the advert in *The Advertiser* by Ellie's ballet teacher, I knew that *Oliver!* would be a fantastic opportunity for her. Neither of us had considered putting her forward for anything in the West End, but this seemed like a great chance to give it a go. The moment I heard she had got in, we were both amazed, but not sure of what was going to be involved and how I was going to fit it in with a busy family and work commitments. The travelling arrangements were made a lot easier for me with the coach which brought them up and back from London. The time distance between the rehearsals and first night seemed surprisingly short.

The day of the opening show, we were all extremely excited. As we pulled up in a taxi outside the theatre, for the first time I went to see Ellie, it suddenly hit me what a big production this was. Seeing her name up on the screen in the foyer made me feel very proud. Schoolwork was a worry to begin with, as we realised the amount of time we would be putting into the show. Her enthusiasm and thrill of performing in the show meant that this was never an issue, and she kept up to date with her work well. It was made clear right from the beginning that she wasn't allowed to miss any school, which was harder for Eleanor with the late nights and early mornings.

Having had the auditions locally, we've made long lasting friendships with other families who were involved in the show and who lived close to us. The show was a big commitment not only for Ellie, but for the whole family, as it meant we were constantly on standby to cover for any absences in the show. Overall we saw Eleanor's confidence and performing skills grow and we are so thankful for this amazing opportunity.'

Jon Lee played *Oliver!* at the London Palladium in 1995. He went on to join S Club Juniors and amongst other roles, as an adult he has played Marius in *Les Misérables* and Frankie Valli in *Jersey Boys*.

Oliver! at the London Palladium was my very first show as Children's Administrator and a 10-year-old Jon Lee auditioned for the title role. He is the only child that has made me cry during an audition. His rendition of 'Where is Love' was absolutely gorgeous. At final casting he auditioned for Sam Mendes, Cameron Mackintosh and Lionel Bart who decided at that stage that he was not right for the part. So he was offered a part in the ensemble instead. At the next set of auditions and soon after Jon had opened in the show as a workhouse boy we decided to present him to Cameron, Sam and Lionel a second time. This time they loved him and he turned out to be one of the best Olivers we had ever had. Jon lived in Devon with his parents at the time and had to move to London to take up the role.

JON'S STORY

'I wasn't majorly disappointed when I didn't get the role straight away. Having had no training or professional experience I was over the moon to be involved in the production in any way I could. Looking back now I don't think I really understood what a big deal it was to be part of the show. To audition for Cameron and Lionel didn't really phase me at the time as I had no idea who they were! I would be extremely nervous if I was put in the same position now.

I think I only performed in the workhouse for a few shows before being asked to audition again, this time being offered the role. This meant I was taken out of the show to preserve the amount of days I was allowed to work. [**Note from the author. In those days children under 13 could only work on forty days in any twelve month period.**] It was such an amazing feeling, I remember phoning my parents and telling them, it was very emotional as you can imagine.

Once I began in the show again I moved up to London where I stayed with Jean Avery [**one of the *Oliver!* chaperones**] for the weeks I was performing and travelled back down to Devon on the weeks I was not. I was going to the Sylvia Young Theatre School whilst in London. I then went on to win the scholarship so stayed up full-time and my parents sold the house and moved up. I always found the initial 'goodbye' to my parents very difficult but once I was at Jean's or at school I was fine. I knew this is what I wanted to do for my career from a very early age and I was thrilled that I was being given such an amazing opportunity. It put me in good stead for later years when I was hardly ever at home.'

Kim Wilson, whose son Ben played Captain in the opening of *Oliver!* at Drury Lane and closed the show as the Artful Dodger. He is a London-based child so did not have to live away.

'If someone had told me when we went for the very first *Oliver!* audition, that my son would still be in it two and a half years later, I would have probably laughed or walked away there and then. I have four children all involved in the performing arts, so life is never dull, someone is always appearing somewhere, but I'd always said being a single parent, that I would never let my child do West End shows mainly because I thought I would never manage it. After seven or eight auditions my son Ben, aged 10, was finally given the part as Captain in the gang. We were all so proud.

I remember lying in bed awake at night wondering how I was ever going to manage the rehearsal schedule, but that was just the start of what became a fantastic couple of years. Ben had such a wonderful time and I must admit so did I. His original gang, The Tanners, very quickly built up a very strong friendship and we still remain friends today, meeting up every couple of months for reunions. Nothing could have prepared me for the opening night and how emotional it was going to be. I really had no idea what to expect, but when he came on that stage, I realized that any fears or worries about whether I was allowing my child to do the right thing, quickly disappeared. You could see how he lit up and I could see he was born to perform. The children in *Oliver!* had such a great time. Night after night it was just like one big party on stage and the camaraderie really shone through.

Ben was very lucky to open the first show as Captain and ended in the very last show as Dodger, the part he longed for from the very beginning. I can't tell you how many times I saw him in the show, but as soon as that opening music played, the tears would stream down my face, and I never got tired of watching it. It just got better and better. The cast of *Oliver!* were brilliant with the children. It was just like one big happy family. During Ben's time in *Oliver!*, he was fortunate to meet many famous stars. His idol, the late Michael Jackson, even came to see the show and that was a night to remember. If you ask Ben how he felt about being on stage, he would just say 'Mum there's nothing like it when you walk on that stage'. He had many late nights and early mornings. He missed lots of school friend's parties and different events but I never heard him complain once. He always got up for school the next morning and managed to stay on target with his school work.

The chaperones were excellent and looked after the children as if they were their own; what a job looking after all those children and always greeting them with a friendly smile or a cuddle when needed. I could go on forever, about what a wonderful time we both had, but I would strongly recommend it to any child, but most of all I would like to thank the casting director Jo Hawes for giving my son the chance of the journey of a lifetime.'

BEN'S VIEW ON HIS AUDITION AND TIME IN *OLIVER!*

'I remember waiting outside for the audition. There were thousands of other children which made me feel very nervous! As I heard my name called to enter the audition it felt as if my stomach leaped out my body I was so nervous… The first audition I got through although then had to go through many other stages. Then one day I remember coming home and my mum was waiting to congratulate me that I had got the role of part of the gang (Captain) in *Oliver!*

A few weeks later we had to start our rehearsals which were very hard work! I remember constantly repeating 'Food Glorious Food'. It was great pretending to be an orphan and having to change emotions from being sad then being the happiest kid in the world. Later on we started the Gang rehearsals which was the funniest thing I've ever done! All of us became brothers and we would always help each other in every way possible. The first show we did was amazing. We had such a good response and so many good reviews! We carried on battling through the shows and were getting better and better! After a while I auditioned for the part of Dodger! I always wished to play The Artful Dodger as Jack Wild was so amazing when he was Dodger and I wanted to be as good as him. Luckily I got the part which was the best news ever! I couldn't imagine going on stage as Dodger but as soon as I got my costume on I wanted to get on stage as soon as possible! I got to perform as Dodger on the last show of *Oliver!* which was an honour and a wonderful experience. Overall I had the most amazing time in *Oliver!* and met so many wonderful people on the journey. I would love to thank everyone who was a part of the *Oliver!* Company although most of all I would like to give the biggest thank you to my mum as she gave me so much support and I couldn't have done it without her!'

Robert Madge played Michael Banks in the very first cast of *Mary Poppins* at the Prince Edward Theatre in London. He lived too far away from London to commute so he lived with a chaperone in the *Oliver!* flat and was educated by private tutor with other 'out of London' children. Once he finished playing Michael Banks (after nearly two years) he went to Sylvia Young's as a boarder. His parents must have especially felt the loss of their son at home as Robert is an only child.

ROBERT'S VIEW

'When I first managed to secure the role of Michael Banks in the West End musical *Mary Poppins* I had no idea what lay ahead. I had just turned nine and when auditioning for the role, I was encouraged by my parents not to raise my hopes. I was an ordinary school boy from a small countryside village in the middle of Leicestershire. My wildest dream of performing on the West End stage seemed a million miles away.

Once I discovered I had gained the role, I found it hard to think that there might be any issues involving this amazing experience. I discovered, soon after, I would have to stay in a flat based in central London with a chaperone: a word I had never come across before. As a boy who felt homesick at the mere thought of sleeping over at my friend's house, who lived just a couple of doors away, this prospect became rather difficult to comprehend. However, with the help of the loving chaperones, friends and other wonderful people I met whilst working on the show, this wasn't an issue. Heather Miller, the head chaperone, in particular, was like a second mum to me! She comforted me on too many occasions. I especially remember how she looked after me on my first night away from home and when I was ill when she fed me hot drinks and endless bowls of chicken soup.

In regards to schooling, I had a full-time tutor Joy Pollard who worked on the show. Joy was wonderful. She taught me everything I needed to know for the whole course of my run in the production, and even helped me prepare for my Year 6 SATS Examinations, for which I gained excellent results, thanks to her. When I was not in London performing, my mother and father home-schooled me, helping me through homework Joy had previously set. This worked well and gave a real advantage in my education.

To conclude, being an actor as a person of my age, things can be difficult but overall if it's what you want to do, go for it! It's an amazing, AMAZING opportunity for anyone, no matter how old they are, and to experience it this young, I think, is a blessing. As Mary Poppins says herself: 'Anything can happen if you let it'.'

JON MADGE – ROBERT'S FATHER

'Robert's first experience of auditions was when he applied for the role of Michael in *Mary Poppins*. I told him he was wasting his time but later that day received a call from Jan saying he'd got a recall. I was convinced we were delaying the inevitable disappointment but Robert proved me wrong and three auditions later he'd got the role!

Once the excitement had settled down we were hit by reality! Robert's rehearsals and performances inevitably involved numerous round trips from our home in the Midlands to London, but this was all worth it when we saw our son on the West End stage for the first time, with a beaming smile on his face!

There were certainly times when we questioned what we'd let ourselves in for; I was abroad with work on Robert's first night away from home. He'd been rehearsing for *Mary Poppins* and had returned to the flat for the evening with Heather. About midnight I received a call from a very homesick little boy, he sobbed and sobbed and had it not been for Heather's love and affection I think I may have flown home immediately. Not enough can be said for the importance of a caring chaperone, Heather was marvellous when Robert was coming to terms with the loss of his Nan, she would talk and listen with great consideration.

Little did we know that this would lead to Robert loving the life so much, that he decided he wanted to apply for a scholarship at the Sylvia Young Theatre School. After challenging auditions and strenuous practices at home, Robert managed to achieve his dream and was awarded a scholarship. This resulted in Robert leaving his home for the week and going to board with a host family in London. Obviously, we have missed Robert during the week but look forward to the weekends when he brightens up the house again! Robert has been almost living away from home since the age of nine, anyway, so we've pretty much got used to it! For anyone whose child aspires to fulfil their dreams in this way, although things can be pretty tough at times, I'd certainly recommend it. It has given us a lot of joy and pleasure and has been worth all the hard work to see Robert achieve his dreams and turn out a rounded, happy individual.'

Aled Jones's daughter Emilia played Princess Fiona in *Shrek* at Drury Lane when it first opened in 2011. For me this is a sharp reminder of how time passes because when I was a stage manager Aled was a boy soprano aged 14 and our paths crossed in Andrew Lloyd Webber's *Requiem* which was performed at the Palace Theatre in London.

Aled talked to me about the various emotions that jostled for position in his mind when he witnessed his daughter in a big production – as a performing child who is now the parent of a performing child he is well aware of the joys and sorrows that may lie ahead. He is quite naturally afraid of her being hurt and certainly does not try to push her into performing. In common with many parents Emilia's parents prepare her for the knocks telling her she probably won't be cast when she goes for auditions. However, being involved in this business is entirely her choice. She appeared in a couple of films prior to being offered *Shrek* and she clearly adores it. She loves the whole experience of being in the theatre, getting ready, the wig, costume, make-up and so on. Her mother tells me that the gaps between performances seem like months to Emilia!

Aled told me he was very emotional during her first performance. He was so proud and at the same time worried that she would forget the words to the song which she sings solo whilst alone onstage. He also helpfully offered tips beforehand such as 'watch the conductor'. Emilia was quite dismissive of any such advice and indeed my impression of her is that she knows exactly what she should be doing!

26

A Final Word!

These days I often receive phone calls from young people asking me for work experience – the 10-year-old boy soprano that had sounded so gorgeous a few years before is now unrecognisable with his broken voice and it just serves to remind me how quickly time passes. I know that it is only a matter of time before I licence a child who is the son or daughter of a previous Jane Banks or Baby Cosette.

I hope that this book is helpful for both parents and children and that it will be a useful point of reference that can be read through and then dipped into as required. I also hope it is entertaining. I thoroughly enjoyed writing it, finding it very interesting to write down 17 years of accumulated knowledge and remembering the various funny incidents that have taken place. Apart from a very few unpleasant incidents there is nothing I would change. This profession is unlike any other and I have never regretted the decision to make it my career.

I passionately believe that children should be given the same opportunity that I have had with lots of informed guidance to help them along the way. I was lucky that I had lots of support from my parents – in particular my father who adored theatre and took me regularly. I did have plenty of resistance from my school, however, which was called The Convent of the Nativity of Our Lord. Convent schools and a future career in theatre are not a good combination: I was told by the nuns that theatre is an immoral profession, I would be out of work most of the time and that I should go to university, read biology and then train to be a nurse. I was strong-minded enough to ignore this very blinkered view of career options, I love nearly every second of my job and over my entire career I have had three months out of work which was my choice.

It is said that we should never work with children or animals. I do not know so much about the animals (although I did once run some auditions to find a whippet for a production of *The Hired Man*) but the children are at once challenging, exasperating and thrilling to watch on stage.

APPENDICES

I. AUDITION FORM

Children's Auditions

PLEASE COMPLETE IN FULL AS CLEARLY AS POSSIBLE	
Name of child	
Home Address	
Postcode	
Name of parent	
Home Telephone number	
Work Telephone number	
Mobile Mum	Dad
Email address	
Date of Birth	AGE
Height in feet and inches	
Education Authority	
i.e the area to which you pay your community charge	
Agency details ~ name	
Telephone number	
Email	
School details ~ name	
Telephone number	
Name of headteacher	
XXXXXXXXXXXXXXXXXXXXXXXXXXXXXXXXXXXXXXXXXXXXXXXXXXXXXXXXXXXXX	
	Please staple small
	photo in this corner
Children must be available from XX to XX – no holidays etc allowed please confirm thank you	
Yes / No	
....	
SIGNED BY PARENT/AGENT ON BEHALF OF THE CHILD	

GENERAL BREAKDOWN

Joanne Hawes

Children's Casting Director

jo.hawes@virgin.net

Current Casting Information

Please read the info below. Please make suggestions on separate emails for each show with the name of the child, dob, age, height and area in which they live i.e their education authority. Please note in all cases boys must have unbroken voices and girls must be undeveloped.

I am unable to help anyone who is too tall or too old for any of these productions and I do not cast adults or have any information about adult casting. So sorry but time does not permit a response to email outside the limits set out below.

All suggestions welcome for all of the shows below providing the children fit the criteria – if they do not I am unable to see them. So sorry but all shows are very specific and the criteria are all there for very good reasons.

Please note that children must be available for the entire time stated as no allowances can be made for holidays or special occasions. We expect 100% commitment whilst the children are in the show.

I am only able to take enquiries by email for reasons of time!

PLEASE NOTE ALL CHILDREN FOR THE PRODUCTIONS BELOW MUST LIVE WITHIN A 45-MILE RADIUS OF LONDON.

Many thanks.

SHREK Theatre Royal Drury Lane

Commitment – six months from September

- YOUNG PRINCESS FIONA – aged 8, a bright little girl, great singing required.
- YOUNG SHREK – also a girl around 8 years old
- Height limit 4' 6" inches for both girls

LES MISÉRABLES Queens Theatre

Commitment – six months from July 2011

- GAVROCHE – Under 4' 7", any nationality, very strong singing and acting.
- Streetwise, tough but likeable kid. About 10 years old, unbroken voice.
- COSETTE – under 4' 4", fair skin, sweet soprano voice.
- EPONINE – who does not sing but she understudies Cosette.

THE LION KING – Cub School Auditions

Every six months

- Height limit 4' 9" and very dark skinned only.
- Children need to be available to attend cub school on Fridays for six months. They are cast to be in the show from cub school only.

I look forward to hearing from you.

Best wishes

Jo

OLIVER! TOUR – BREAKDOWN

DATES: October 2010 in London Opening in Cardiff December 2011

REQUIREMENTS

OLIVER – Around 10 years old and no taller than 4' 7", fairish, fabulous treble singing, unbroken voice, vulnerable but tough and feisty. Oliver does not really dance but must be coordinated.

THE ARTFUL DODGER – Maximum height 5 feet, excellent singing and dancing required, unbroken voice, a big character.

GANG – Maximum height 5 feet, excellent singing and dancing required, unbroken voice, all have their own character and range in age from 7 (Nipper) to 14 (Charlie Bates).

BET – Bet is played by an adult.

- All of the above parts are played by boys only.
- All nationalities, skin colour etc are welcome.
- No fixed braces.
- Boys will tour with the show for nine months – on a rota.
- Rehearsals will be in London and all boys must be London based for logistical reasons. Please bear that in mind before putting children forward.
- Before making submissions please be sure that schools are fully aware of the commitment and prepared to give permission.
- Please be sure that parents are aware of the huge commitment also. They will be expected to commute to the rehearsal room

most days and once performances start they will drop their sons at the most convenient London station to meet the chaperones.

ENSEMBLE CHILDREN

Two or three teams of ten ensemble children will be cast locally to perform for a few weeks on a rota in their local venue. These auditions will be held in the venue itself over a weekend and will be completely separate from the London auditions.

- All children will be local to the venue – within 25 miles.
- They will be brought backwards and forwards by their parents but we will chaperone in the theatre / rehearsal room.
- They must be available for the dates above plus rehearsal prior to opening.
- These children play various parts in many of the numbers in the show but are not part of the gang.
- They are boys and girls.
- They are all under 5 feet.
- They all have unbroken voices.
- They are all nationalities.
- They are not younger than 8 and not older than 13.
- They are undeveloped.
- They sing and dance well.

VENUES THAT WE WILL BE VISITING ARE:

- Cardiff   December 2011 – January 2012
- Manchester   January – March 2012
- Birmingham   March – April
- Southampton   April – May
- Edinburgh   May – June

- Norwich   July
- Plymouth   August – September
- Newcastle   September – October
- Leeds   November – December
- Dublin   December – January 2013
- Bristol   January – February
- Tour closes

I look forward to hearing from you. Please email only ~ no photos required.

When emailing please include the following:

Name

Age / dob

Education authority

Height

Confirmation that school and parents are aware of the commitment and our expectations.

Please make suggestions for gang boys on one email.

Any local children should be suggested on separate emails for each venue so that I can file them away as appropriate.

Many thanks

Jo

Jo.hawes@virgin.net

2. RECALL LETTER

A UK TOUR

Joanne Hawes ~ Children's Administrator

Email: jo.hawes@virgin.net

Dear

CONGRATULATIONS! We would like to invite you to a recall.

DATE:

VENUE:

TIME:

In the afternoon there will be a further recall for some children from 2–5. This will be final casting we hope. Parents must wait all the time. Please bring food for your young actors!

REMINDERS

- If you are offered a part the commitment will be from X until sometime in Y. The children live at home while rehearsing in London and tour three days on and six days off while performing. They will stay in first-class hotels with chaperones and will be tutored whilst away. We do not tour parents under any circumstances.
- It is vital that you have school support.
- Please bring a passport photo with you to the recall.
- Please note that no time off is permitted during the contract for holidays or special occasions.
- Please practice the material from the show that you have been taught today.
- Please make sure you know the dialogue but do not allow anyone to coach you in how to say it. This can cause serious problems later if you have to 'unlearn' something!
- Please do not hesitate to contact me (by email) if you have any queries.

Finally may I wish you the very best of luck and say that we look forward to seeing you again.

Best wishes

Jo

3. FEEDBACK ABOUT THE AUDITION CLASSES

Thank you for the workshop yesterday, my daughters found it most informative.

Would just like to say that Emily enjoyed your workshop very much, she said she wished it would have been longer as she had so much fun and learnt some good audition techniques.

Thank you for the audition masterclass you held in Manchester today. I really enjoyed myself and learnt lots of useful information and tips to help me in any future auditions which I attend.

A quick thanks for a great class this morning – well worth the trip from Bournemouth! Was thoroughly enjoyed by both girls – look forward to any more you may run in the future.

Thank you for giving your time to provide such an important insight for all the youngsters.

It was a useful 90 minutes and I learned a lot from it.

Just to let you know that after attending one of your art of auditioning classes I was successful in gaining a place at Tring Park School for the Performing Arts.

Just to say my children really loved your workshop yesterday. M. was positively buzzing with excitement over it.

Just a quick note to say L. thoroughly enjoyed the class yesterday, it was well worth the journey; it took 90+ minutes each way, but he was so pleased he came. He read the little book cover to cover on the way home, then passed it to me to read my section. It was great, especially as he appeared to be in the minority in that he didn't know anyone else; but then I believe that helps their confidence in itself.

ACKNOWLEDGEMENTS

I would like to thank my publisher, Andrew Walby, for his belief and for commissioning this book in the first place – it has been great fun to write.

Thanks also to Sir Cameron Mackintosh, Edward Snape of Fiery Angel, and Denise Wood at the Royal Shakespeare Company, for kindly allowing me to reproduce the logos for *Oliver!*, *Mary Poppins*, *Les Misérables*, *Goodnight Mr Tom* and *Matilda: The Musical*.

Grateful thanks to Aled Jones, Eleanor and Ros Duncombe, Ben and Kim Wilson, Robert and John Madge and also Jon Lee for sharing their thoughts for inclusion in the book.

A big thank you to Merlyn Viner for painstakingly correcting the text on holiday. Also to Ian Hart for correcting one or two leagalities and always being an excellent sounding board.

To all the producers, directors, choreographers, musical directors, agents, chaperones, parents and children who have provided me with the experiences without which there would be no book, I thank you too.

But the biggest thanks of all is to Tim.

Jo Hawes, December 2011

WWW.OBERONBOOKS.COM

 Follow us on www.twitter.com/@oberonbooks
& www.facebook.com/oberonbook